PROGRAMMING LANGUAGE TRANSLATION

SERIES IN COMPUTERS AND THEIR APPLICATIONS

Series Editor: BRIAN MEEK

Director of the Computer Unit, Queen Elizabeth College, University of London

The series aims to provide up-to-date and readable texts on the theory and practice of computing, with particular though not exclusive emphasis on computer applications. Preference is given in planning the series to new or developing areas, or to new approaches in established areas.

The books will usually be at the level of introductory or advanced undergraduate courses. In most cases they will be suitable as course texts, with their use in industrial and commercial fields always kept in mind. Together they will provide a valuable nucleus for a computing science library.

PROGRAMMING LANGUAGE TRANSLATION

R. E. BERRY, B.Sc., M.Sc.
Department of Computer Studies
University of Lancaster

ELLIS HORWOOD LIMITED
Publishers · Chichester

Halsted Press: a division of
JOHN WILEY & SONS
New York · Brisbane · Chichester · Toronto

First published in 1982 by
Reprinted in 1983
ELLIS HORWOOD LIMITED
Market Cross House, Cooper Street, Chichester, West Sussex, PO19 1EB, England

The publisher's colophon is reproduced from James Gillison's drawing of the ancient Market Cross, Chichester.

Distributors:

Australia, New Zealand, South-east Asia:
Jacaranda-Wiley Ltd., Jacaranda Press,
JOHN WILEY & SONS INC.,
G.P.O. Box 859, Brisbane, Queensland 40001, Australia

Canada:
JOHN WILEY & SONS CANADA LIMITED
22 Worcester Road, Rexdale, Ontario, Canada.

Europe, Africa:
JOHN WILEY & SONS LIMITED
Baffins Lane, Chichester, West Sussex, England.

North and South America and the rest of the world:
Halsted Press: a division of
JOHN WILEY & SONS
605 Third Avenue, New York, N.Y. 10016, U.S.A.

© **1981 R. E. Berry/Ellis Horwood Limited.**

British Library Cataloguing in Publication Data
Berry, R. E.
Programming language translation. —
(Ellis Horwood series in computers and their applications)
1. Compiling (Electronic computers)
I. Title
001.64'25   QA76.6

Library of Congress Card No. 81–13469 AACR2

ISBN 0–85312–379–9 (Ellis Horwood Limited – Library Edn.)
ISBN 0–85312–430–2 (Ellis Horwood Limited – Student Edn.)
ISBN 0–470–27305–4 (Halsted Press)

Typeset in Press Roman by Ellis Horwood Ltd.
Printed in Great Britain by R. J. Acford, Chichester.

Table of Contents

Author's Preface

This book provides an introduction to some of the more important techniques used in the construction of program translators. The book is directed at the increasing number of computer users who are curious to know more about the compilers or assemblers which process their programs. This has led me to write an overview, rather than an exhaustive study, of particular topics. As a source of examples I have made considerable use of Pascal S. Most if not all Pascal compilers are written in Pascal. While this property of being written in the language they compile is not exclusive to Pascal compilers, it makes them invaluable in teaching. I have used Pascal S in teaching for a number of years in different environments and its value as a teaching vehicle has become apparent through the interest it arouses in students. A listing of the Pascal S compiler/ interpreter is provided, and I am grateful to Professor N. Wirth for permission to include this.

My thanks are due to my wife, and to the colleagues and students who have, directly or indirectly, helped in the preparation of this material. The responsibility for it is, however, mine alone. The series editor Brian Meek also deserves special thanks for his careful, pertinent, and helpful comments on my early manuscript.

Introduction

A program translator accepts as input a program written by a user and produces as output a version of that program which can be directly or indirectly executed by a computer. This translation process will include verifying that the user's program does not violate the syntax rules of the language in which it is written, checking that all symbols defined by the user are used in a consistent way, and generating a version of the program suitable for execution or interpretation. The user expects the translation process to produce a program which, when executed, will have the same effect as his original program were it directly executable. The translation from one program form to another is a complex task. Too often it is described by enumerating the techniques necessary to accomplish it with little attempt to identify the inter-relationships of these techniques. In an attempt to avoid this pitfall I shall discuss various aspects of the translation process and identify their implementation in a specific translator, the Pascal S compiler. To lend emphasis to this approach I have divided the book into two parts. Part 1 considers translation in general, but both text and examples progressively assume familiarity with the compiler given in part two. Part 2 gives a listing and documentation of the Pascal S compiler. Both parts assume familiarity with Pascal.

Pascal S is a subset of Pascal. In consequence the Pascal S compiler is small in comparison with many of the Pascal compilers currently in use. Nonetheless, significant effort is required to gain an insight into the compiler's action by studying its listing and such documentary help as is given here. This effort is well rewarded if it helps the reader understand a complex and important piece of software.

PART 1

Chapter 1
Lexical Analysis

1.1 USER INTERFACE

In considering the work of a compiler or an assembler it is too easy to assume that all such items behave in the same manner as those with which the reader is familiar. A user could communicate with these items of system software in several ways. Cards, paper tape, and interactive terminals may all be used to prepare a program which is subsequently submitted for processing. Further, cards may be encoded in different ways, paper tape may appear in different sizes (8 track, 7 track and currently the less common 5 track) as well as with different encodings, whilst terminals may transmit a line at a time or a character at a time for processing. Whatever the media selected, the user is simply trying to present his program for processing and can legitimately expect that the form of input media he chooses should not affect the integrity of his program. Equally, much of a compiler's effort is directed to determining whether the program submitted for processing is a valid program according to the rules of the programming language used. This judgement must be made whatever input medium was used. It will, I hope, be clear to the reader that accepting one character at a time from an interactive terminal will mean recognising *rub-outs* or perhaps *backspaces* as deleting the preceding character, whereas accepting a line at a time should mean that no such deletion characters are ever transmitted.

Some of the problems in dealing with a wide range of input media are dealt with in Hopgood and Bell [5] .

1.2 ALPHABET

From this point it will be assumed that we have access to a character stream which is free of the idiosyncrasies of any data preparation device. But before proceeding further we need to establish what characters will be considered as legal input for processing. For example a Fortran compiler must flag the character '[' as illegal, since no use is made of it in Fortran. Is the compiler to accept upper and lower case letters? Should a Pascal compiler accept the character '{'

as well as the character pair '(*' to denote the opening of a comment? These questions must be resolved in order that all characters which do not form part of the legitimate input to a compiler can be identified and flagged as erroneous. Having identified the character set or alphabet we are prepared to deal with, it is then legitimate to ask what we are to do with these characters.

In lexical analysis we consider the user's source program simply as a character stream. We must scan this input stream in order to find groups of characters which may be called *textual elements*. These are words, punctuation, single and multi-character operators, comments, spaces etc. which comprise the user's program. In its simplest form the scanner (lexical analyser) finds these groups of characters and classifies each according to its textual element, and passes on a much reduced form of the original program for subsequent processing. In particular, comments which are recognised are eliminated. Spaces, line feeds, carriage returns and other editing symbols once recognised have no further value and are also eliminated. It is important to note however that spaces may play an important role, since in some languages, notably PL/1 and Cobol, they have the role of delimiters. That is, they mark the end of such textual units as reserved words. Most if not all implementations of Pascal adopt this approach. In other language implementations, reserved words may be preceded and followed by a special character other than space.

For example begin appears as 'begin' in many implementations of Algol 60 and Algol 68. Whatever delimiters are used, it will be the function of the scanner to collect the characters between consecutive delimiters, of which the space character is only one, and to determine whether this group of characters is a textual unit, and if so what kind. Once recognised as a valid textual unit each group of characters is replaced by a token or internal symbol which is used for easier recognition in subsequent processing. The precise form this token takes is a matter for a particular implementor, but it can take the form of a reference to a particular table together with a position number, or a special bit pattern in a byte or a word, or, as in the case of Pascal S, it can be given the value of an element in a set of predefined symbols. In order to help clarify the role of the token, consider the programming language statement:

$$\underline{if}\ x > y\ \underline{then}\ x := x - y\ \underline{else}\ y := y - x$$

The language presents the statement in this form because it is readable and easily intelligible to users. The same statement could equally be written in the form:

$$|\ x > y \sim x \backslash x - y\ @\ y \backslash y - x$$

which is perhaps not quite so easily understood. All that has happened is that the compound symbols of the first example (i.e. if, then, else, :=) which consist of more than one character, have been replaced by single character equivalents in the second example. In short, the reserved words have been replaced by tokens. For this example tokens are visual, but for our scanner they clearly need not be.

The recognition of such textual units and their replacement by tokens implies that we can recognise any one of the possible reserved words. This will mean that the scanner must have access to a list of all reserved words and can correctly identify a group of characters as being one item from this list. This involves a *table look-up* which may be undertaken in several different ways. For the moment we shall take it that the look-up can be done and postpone a discussion of how until later. Hence we can assume that we have reduced each reserved word to a simple token.

One item which can be dealt with in a straightforward manner for many high level languages is the string. If we consider the Pascal statement:

write ('this is a string')

then the collection of items between apostrophes is a string. It is usually of no importance what characters or how many characters are in the string since in most languages such strings cannot be manipulated. Accordingly a scanner, having successfully recognised such a string, is likely to store away the string in, say, a string table, and leave a token in the program source which will denote the presence of a string and where it may be located.

The textual units which occur most frequently in the user's source program will be identifiers, or user-defined symbols. Such identifiers will range from one character to some implementation- or language-defined maximum number of characters in length. Since in the remainder of the compiler it will be time consuming to be constantly dealing with multi-character identifiers, it is useful to cause the scanner to construct a table of all the identifiers which are recognised, and to replace them in the user's source program by a token, together with sufficient information to locate the appropriate symbol in the identifier table. Note that, for the reserved words of the language, the scanner attempted to look up the appropriate group of characters in a previously constructed table, while in the case of identifiers a slightly different operation is required. The identifier table (or that part of it to which we currently have access) must first be scanned to see if an entry already exists for this group of characters. If it does, well and good; if it does not then an entry must be created.

Apart from symbols such as ':=', '..', which, although consisting of more than one character, are easily dealt with because they are few in number and can be treated as special cases, the only multi-character textual units which have not been dealt with are numeric constants.

Numeric constants divide into two types, those with fractional parts and those without. It is the scanner's function to recognise valid representations of each within the source program being processed. This can often be done by making use of a *state table*. It will be instructive to consider an example of this technique but in order to do so at this point we need to anticipate material which will be covered in more detail later. In particular it is assumed that the reader is familiar with definitions given in the following form:

⟨ unsigned number ⟩ ::=   digit ⟨ rest unsigned number ⟩

⟨ unsigned number ⟩ ::=   . ⟨ decimal fraction ⟩

⟨ unsigned number ⟩ ::=   E ⟨ exponent part ⟩

⟨ rest unsigned number ⟩ ::=   digit ⟨ rest unsigned number ⟩

⟨ rest unsigned number ⟩ ::=   . ⟨ decimal fraction ⟩

⟨ rest unsigned number ⟩ ::=   E ⟨ exponent part ⟩

⟨ rest unsigned number ⟩ ::=   ⟂

⟨ decimal fraction ⟩ ::=   digit ⟨ rest decimal fraction ⟩

⟨ rest decimal fraction ⟩ ::=   ⟂

⟨ rest decimal fraction ⟩ ::=   E ⟨exponent part ⟩

⟨ rest decimal fraction ⟩ ::=   digit ⟨ rest decimal fraction ⟩

⟨ exponent part ⟩ ::=   sign ⟨ exponent integer ⟩

⟨ exponent part ⟩ ::=   digit ⟨ rest exponent integer ⟩

⟨ exponent enteger ⟩ ::=   digit ⟨ rest exponent integer ⟩

⟨ rest exponent integer ⟩ ::=   digit ⟨ rest exponent integer ⟩

⟨ rest exponent integer ⟩ ::=   ⟂

This is not the most compact way of expressing these definitions but in this form their use in constructing a table is most easily seen. Notice that there are seven different items enclosed in angle brackets, and that each of these appears at least once on the left hand side of the definitions listed. These items:

1   unsigned number

2   rest unsigned number

3   decimal fraction

4   rest decimal fraction

5   exponent part

6   exponent integer

7   rest exponent integer

determine the number of states, or rows in the table, while the number of columns is determined by the number of terminal symbols or characters we need to use in the definitions listed. Note that nothing is lost by regarding ⟨ sign ⟩ and

⟨digit⟩ as terminal symbols. The symbol —△— is used to represent any other character. With this information the table which may be used by the scanner is now constructed.

	Sign	digit	·	E	△
1	/	2	3	5	/
2	/	2	3	5	exit
3	/	4	/	/	/
4	/	4	/	5	exit
5	6	7	/	/	/
6	/	7	/	/	/
7	/	7	/	/	exit

The first row is the entry for ⟨unsigned number⟩, and in the list of defining rules this item appears three times on the left hand side of a definition. The corresponding right hand sides require that 'digit', '·', 'E' are recognised and accordingly there are entries in the first row of the table for the elements with these characters at the head of the column. In each case the entry is the row number of the item in angle brackets which follows the character in the appropriate definition. Thus in the first row under E the entry is 5 which refers to the fifth row and thus the item in angle brackets with reference 5, i.e. exponent part.

Use of the table is straightforward, since all that is required is that the current state (row number) and current character from the input stream be available. This information is used to determine an element position in the table which will be the new state or row number. Starting at state 1 it can be seen that only those characters which can be legitimately expected at that point in the processing will produce a satisfactory change of state. Any other character will take us to a table entry containing / which can be regarded as an error exit. As long as the definition of floating point constant in the language being processed can be redefined in the form of a set of rules such as those given earlier, this technique may be used. This is efficient and can produce good diagnostics though it does need table space.

Let us take 3.141* as the character string to be parsed. The start state is 1, and the first character is a digit. Inspection of the first row of the state table shows that the new state is to be 2. In this state we consider the next character of the input string which is the decimal point. The entry under the decimal point in the second row of the state table is 3, which is the new state. This process can be more concisely represented by the following table:

current state	current character	new state
1	3	2
2	.	3
3	1	4
4	4	4
4	1	4
4	*	exit

The sole purpose of the finite state table is to help the scanner recognise a particular item. The result of using the table in the example as described would be to produce a simple *yes* or *no* answer to the question *was the number processed a valid floating point number?*. A scanner will frequently combine recognition of such an item with its evaluation and conversion to an *internal form*. However, if this additional work is undertaken then one must make assumptions about the computer on which the compiler is to run. This is because the way in which a floating point number is stored will vary from machine to machine. As a result there are persuasive arguments for postponing such conversion operations until later in the compilation process so that as much of the compiler as possible can be made independent of particular machines. As far as our scanner is concerned it will be sufficient to assume that successful recognition of a floating point number will cause its replacement by a suitable token and table reference. It should be clear that integer constants can be dealt with by the table constructed, though they too will be unsigned constants.

The role of the scanner can be regarded as that of accepting the character stream as input, which is the user's source program, and producing as output a string much reduced in length and consisting of a series of tokens, together with one or more tables. However, this simple view comes from looking at the scanner in isolation. In practice, the scanner is more likely to be invoked as and when required by other elements of the compilation process. This can be clearly seen by considering the roles of nextch and insymbol in the Pascal S compiler.

EXERCISES

1. Identify, and list the differences between, the floating point numbers accepted by the finite state recogniser in the text, and the floating point numbers defined in the Pascal S syntax diagrams.

2. Describe which tokens, if any, the Pascal S compiler uses for each of the following symbols $':='$, $'<>'$, $'..'$, $'(*'$, $'<='$.

3. Operands of an expression may be single digits, or single characters. The permitted operators are +, −, *, /,. Construct a finite state recogniser for expressions which do not contain a unary operator, and also one for expressions which may contain a unary operator.

4. Is a comment within a comment legal in Pascal S? What is the outcome if a program with such a construction is processed by the compiler?

5. List the modifications necessary to the Pascal S compiler in order that both upper and lower case characters may be used for input. The modifications should ensure that, for example, BeGIN will be correctly recognised.

Chapter 2

Syntax Definition and Syntax Analysis

In writing a computer program a user must use a programming language. Such languages have only been available since about 1950. They have been designed by man for his own use. Our natural language has evolved over many hundreds of years and, comparing these timescales, it should come as no surprise that programming languages are not yet so rich nor perhaps as flexible as we would like. Nonetheless, programming languages have reached the stage where much use is made of them, and features which are hard to implement or hard to use now rarely pass the design stage of the language.

When designing a language, serious consideration must be given to the character set to be used, the ways in which these characters can be combined to make symbols, and the rules which govern how these symbols may be combined to produce the *sentences* of the language. There are a variety of ways in which a compiler may verify that a program is syntactically correct; that is, correctly constructed according to the rules of the language being used. It will be instructive to examine how the rules which govern the syntax of a language may be expressed. Consider the following rules:

1. ⟨ number ⟩ ::= ⟨ num ⟩

2. ⟨ num ⟩ ::= ⟨ num ⟩⟨ digit ⟩ | ⟨ digit ⟩

3. ⟨ digit ⟩ ::= 0 | 1 | 2 | 3 | 4 | 5 | 6 | 7 | 8 | 9 |

note that rule 2 can be written more concisely as:

⟨ num ⟩ ::= ⟨ digit ⟩ {⟨ digit ⟩}

Rule 3 simply defines an item called ⟨digit⟩ which is one of the characters 0 to 9. Remember the purpose of the rules is to define rigorously and concisely how new symbols may be constructed. For this purpose no reliance can be placed on intuitive notions of what a digit, or for that matter a number, shall be. Rule 2 gives two alternatives for how a num can be formed. It may simply be a digit, or it may be a num (therefore a digit) followed by a digit. In short a num may consist of one or many digits. The first rule simply states that number is a num. The items in angle brackets are non-terminals and the digits themselves are terminals, i.e. characters which could be recognised by a program. Our three rules comprise a grammar for the definition of number. They are rules of the grammar and are frequently known as production rules, because they indicate what needs to be done to produce the item on the left hand side of a rule. This way of expressing the rules of a grammar is known as the Backus Naur form (BNF) and has, together with some of its variants, been widely used in the literature on computing. In the report defining Pascal [6] Wirth uses both BNF and syntax diagrams to define the Pascal grammar. Thus a user can judge the relative merits of each form of definition for particular language constructs.

The purpose of both methods of expressing grammatical rules is to define for the user the ways in which he can combine the elements of a language. However we are faced in a compiler with the problem of examining a sequence of symbols and attempting to determine whether such a sequence could have been produced legitimately using the rules of the grammar. If the answer is *yes* then the program is valid, otherwise it is not. Remembering that in the lexical analysis such items as reserved words, identifiers, and numeric constants were replaced by tokens or single symbols, attention can now be focused upon whether the resulting combination of tokens constitutes a valid program.

At this point we can follow Gries [1] (section 2.4) and consider a syntax tree associated with the rules of the grammar for ⟨number⟩. From this grammar we may derive the following

⟨ number ⟩	—> ⟨ num ⟩	(rule 1
⟨ num ⟩	—> ⟨ num ⟩ ⟨ digit ⟩	(rule 2
	—> ⟨ digit ⟩ ⟨ digit ⟩	(rule 2
	—> 3 ⟨ digit ⟩	(rule 3
	—> 3 4	(rule 3

reading —> as 'produces')

This shows that 34 is a number which can be generated from the rules of the grammar. This derivation can be represented diagrammatically as shown in Figure 2.1.

This is constructed by drawing a vertical line downwards when a rule requires the simple replacement of one item by another whether or not it is an angle bracket. Using the first alternative of rule 2 requires that one item (⟨num⟩) is replaced by two items (⟨num⟩ ⟨digit⟩). In this case the horizontal line is used to *link* the two items. The resulting diagram is a *syntax tree*. A *branch* of this tree is the set of lines together with nodes (the symbols) below these lines. The *end nodes* are those nodes which have no branches below them. The end nodes, reading from left to right, form the string derived from the application of

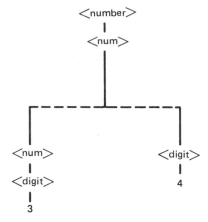

Fig. 2.1 – A simple syntax tree.

rules which the tree represents (34 in the above example). What we are attempting to do in the syntax analysis phase of the compilation is to establish whether the string of symbols being processed can be produced by applying the rules of the grammar of the programming language. In order to establish this we could proceed in two different ways. We could start at the top of the tree and attempt, by rigorously applying the rules of the grammar, to produce exactly the same string of symbols we have been given. The second method takes quite the opposite approach and considers the string of symbols and seeks to recognise groups of them which can be identified as the right hand side of one of the rules of the grammar. If this can be done, then such groups are reduced to (replaced by) the symbol on the left hand side of the appropriate rule. By repeated application of this reduction process we should ultimately be left with a single symbol. The first method is termed top down. or descending analysis. The second method is called bottom up, or ascending analysis. The reason for these names can be seen by looking at the syntax tree. Both methods have been extensively used in compilers, and techniques for their implementation have improved considerably in recent years. Since the Pascal S compiler uses top down analysis and will receive more discussion later, let us briefly consider what is involved in implementing a bottom up analysis using the following grammar from Bolliett [7]

$$\langle p \rangle :: = \langle b \rangle$$
$$\langle b \rangle :: = 1 : \langle b \rangle \mid \langle n \rangle \mid s$$
$$\langle n \rangle :: = \langle t \rangle; \langle f \rangle$$
$$\langle t \rangle :: = \underline{begin}\, d \mid \langle t \rangle; d$$
$$\langle f \rangle :: = \langle b \rangle; \langle f \rangle \mid \langle b \rangle\, \underline{end}$$

where to make the grammar more intelligible we may assume

⟨ p ⟩ is program
⟨ b ⟩ is block
⟨ n ⟩ is unlabelled block
⟨ t ⟩ is head of block
⟨ f ⟩ is end of block

The terminal symbols (those we expect to find in the input stream) are <u>begin</u>, <u>end</u>, 1 (label), d (declaration), s (statement). Since we are attempting to recognise the right hand sides of our rules in order to reduce them to the single symbol of the left hand side, it is convenient to rewrite the rules in the following way:

1.	⟨ b ⟩	=>	⟨ p ⟩
2.	1 : ⟨ b ⟩	=>	⟨ b ⟩
3.	⟨ n ⟩	=>	⟨ b ⟩
4.	⟨ t ⟩; d	=>	⟨ t ⟩
4a.	⟨ t ⟩; ⟨ f ⟩	=>	⟨ n ⟩
5.	begin d	=>	⟨ t ⟩
6.	⟨ b ⟩; ⟨ f ⟩	=>	⟨ f ⟩
6a.	⟨ b ⟩ end	=>	⟨ f ⟩
7.	s	=>	⟨ b ⟩

Note that even in this limited grammar two rules have the same two symbols (⟨ t ⟩;) at the start of the sequence we are to identify. In practice this is a common occurrence, and in order to overcome this problem and others which could lead to the selection of the *wrong* reduction, use is made of a successor matrix. Our goal is of course to establish that we have recognised a program (⟨ p ⟩) and in order to do this successfully a variety of sub-goals must be reached en route. Accordingly the function of the successor matrix is to cause us only to perform those reductions which will lead to the current sub-goal.

	p	b	n	t	f
p	/	/	/	/	/
b	t	/	/	/	t
n	t	t	/	/	t
t	t	t	t	t	t
f	/	/	/	/	/
1	t	t	/	/	t
s	t	t	/	/	t
begin	t	t	t	t	t
d	/	/	/	/	/
end	/	/	/	/	/
:	/	/	/	/	/
;	/	/	/	/	/

Note: t = true.

"The matrix of successors specifies for each symbol (row headers), terminal or nonterminal, whether or not the application of a rule beginning with this symbol can lead to the final or intermediate goal (column header) under consideration". Bolliet [7].

A bottom up analysis of the string

1 : <u>begin</u> d ;d ;<u>begin</u> d ;s <u>end</u> <u>end</u>

using the tables and rules given is illustrated below. The rightmost symbol of the input string is the *current* symbol, and the rightmost symbol in the goal column is the top of the goal stack. It is assumed that whenever a sub-goal is pushed onto the stack, information about the current state of the analysis is also kept. This means that the analysis can be resumed by returning to this state when the sub goal has been reached. At step 1 our goal is ⟨p⟩, the current input symbol is '1'. The only rule starting with '1' is rule 2 and therefore the analysis starts by trying to recognise in the input string the symbols which form this rule.

Step	Input string	Goal stack	Rule
1	1	⟨p⟩	2 1:⟨b⟩
			↑
2	1:	⟨p⟩	2 1:⟨b⟩
			↑

both '1' and the following colon can be found in the input string

3	1 : <u>begin</u>	⟨p⟩	2 1:⟨b⟩
			↑

the input symbol which follows ':' does not match the corresponding symbol in the rule. The rule requires a non-terminal symbol, ⟨b⟩, as the next component. Using the successor matrix we ask whether the goal ⟨b⟩ can be achieved by a rule starting with the current input symbol <u>begin</u>. The answer is *yes*, and so we adopt ⟨b⟩ as a goal and look for a rule starting with <u>begin</u>.

4	1 : <u>begin</u>	⟨p⟩⟨b⟩	5 <u>begin</u> d
			↑
5	1 : <u>begin</u>	⟨p⟩⟨b⟩	5 <u>begin</u> d
			↑

The last symbol of rule 5 matches the current input symbol. We have recognised ⟨t⟩. The part of the input string which corresponds to the left hand side of rule 5 is replaced by the right hand side of rule 5. That is we *reduce* <u>begin</u> d to ⟨t⟩· However our goal is ⟨b⟩. Can we reach this goal with a rule starting with ⟨t⟩?

Using the successor matrix it can be seen that the answer is *yes* and so we continue by finding a rule starting with ⟨t⟩.

6.	1:⟨t⟩;	⟨p⟩⟨b⟩	4⟨t⟩;d ↑
7.	1:⟨t⟩;d	⟨p⟩⟨b⟩	4⟨t⟩;d ↑

Another ⟨t⟩ has been recognised and as before we make a reduction. This ⟨t⟩ does not match our goal but will lead to it. To continue we find a rule starting with ⟨t⟩.

8	1:⟨t⟩;	⟨p⟩⟨b⟩	4⟨t⟩;d ↑
9	1:⟨t⟩; <u>begin</u>	⟨p⟩⟨b⟩	4⟨t⟩;d ↑

A mismatch occurs. The input symbol is <u>begin</u> but rule 4 requires 'd'. Rule 4 does not represent this part of the input string. Is there an alternative? At step 8, where rule 4 was selected, a rule starting with ⟨t⟩ was needed. Rule 4a also starts with ⟨t⟩ and so analysis restarts from step 8 and the new step is designated 8'.

8'	1:⟨t⟩;	⟨p⟩⟨b⟩	4a⟨t⟩; ⟨f⟩ ↑
9'	1:⟨t⟩; <u>begin</u>	⟨p⟩⟨b⟩	4a⟨t⟩; ⟨f⟩ ↑

Once more the current input symbol does not match the symbol of the rule being followed. However in this case the rule symbol is a non-terminal and so, since the current input symbol can lead to this non-terminal, we adopt the non-terminal as a new sub goal, and find a rule which starts with the current input symbol.

10	1:⟨t⟩; <u>begin</u>	⟨p⟩⟨b⟩⟨f⟩	5 <u>begin</u> d ↑
11	1:⟨t⟩; <u>begin</u> d	⟨p⟩⟨b⟩⟨f⟩	5 <u>begin</u> d ↑

Part of the input string now matches rule 5 and can thus be reduced to ⟨t⟩. Since ⟨t⟩ can lead to ⟨f⟩ a rule starting with ⟨t⟩ is found.

12	1:⟨t⟩;⟨t⟩; ⟨p⟩⟨b⟩⟨f⟩ 4⟨t⟩;d

$\qquad\qquad\qquad\qquad\qquad\qquad\qquad\qquad\qquad\qquad\qquad\qquad\uparrow$

13	1:⟨t⟩;⟨t⟩;s ⟨p⟩⟨b⟩⟨f⟩ 4⟨t⟩;d

$\qquad\qquad\qquad\qquad\qquad\qquad\qquad\qquad\qquad\qquad\qquad\qquad\uparrow$

A mismatch is detected. Try an alternative to rule 4 at step 12.

12′   1:⟨t⟩;⟨t⟩;   ⟨p⟩⟨b⟩⟨f⟩   4a⟨t⟩;⟨f⟩
$\qquad\qquad\qquad\qquad\qquad\qquad\qquad\qquad\qquad\qquad\qquad\qquad\uparrow$

13′   1:⟨t⟩;⟨t⟩;s   ⟨p⟩⟨b⟩⟨f⟩   4a⟨t⟩;⟨f⟩
$\qquad\qquad\qquad\qquad\qquad\qquad\qquad\qquad\qquad\qquad\qquad\qquad\uparrow$

The current input symbol does not match the correponding rule element. The rule element ⟨f⟩ is a non-terminal and, since ′s′ can lead to ⟨f⟩, ⟨f⟩ becomes a new goal.

14   1:⟨t⟩;⟨t⟩;s   ⟨p⟩⟨b⟩⟨f⟩⟨f⟩ 7 s
$\qquad\qquad\qquad\qquad\qquad\qquad\qquad\qquad\qquad\qquad\qquad\uparrow$

Input symbol ′s′ matches rule 7 and so is reduced to ⟨b⟩. A new rule starting with ⟨b⟩ is selected.

15   1:⟨t⟩;⟨t⟩;⟨b⟩
            <u>end</u>
                       ⟨p⟩⟨b⟩⟨f⟩⟨f⟩ 6⟨b⟩;⟨f⟩
$\qquad\qquad\qquad\qquad\qquad\qquad\qquad\qquad\qquad\qquad\qquad\uparrow$

The rule symbol does not match the input symbol. An alternative rule is chosen.

15′   1:⟨t⟩;⟨t⟩;⟨b⟩
             <u>end</u>   ⟨p⟩⟨b⟩⟨f⟩⟨f⟩ 6a⟨b⟩<u>end</u>
$\qquad\qquad\qquad\qquad\qquad\qquad\qquad\qquad\qquad\qquad\qquad\uparrow$

Goal ⟨f⟩ is achieved. Remove ⟨f⟩ from the goal stack and resume analysis from step 13′ where the goal ⟨f⟩ was stacked.

16   1:⟨t⟩;⟨t⟩;⟨f⟩ ⟨p⟩⟨b⟩⟨f⟩   4a⟨t⟩;⟨f⟩
$\qquad\qquad\qquad\qquad\qquad\qquad\qquad\qquad\qquad\qquad\qquad\uparrow$

Reduce to ⟨n⟩ using rule 4a.

17   1:⟨t⟩;⟨n⟩   ⟨p⟩⟨b⟩⟨f⟩   3⟨n⟩
$\qquad\qquad\qquad\qquad\qquad\qquad\qquad\qquad\qquad\uparrow$

Reduce to ⟨b⟩ using rule 3.

    18   1:⟨t⟩;⟨b⟩ end ⟨p⟩⟨b⟩⟨f⟩   6⟨b⟩;⟨f⟩
                                                            ↑

The mismatch is detected. Choose an alternative rule.

    18′   1:⟨t⟩;⟨b⟩ end ⟨p⟩⟨b⟩⟨f⟩   6a⟨b⟩ end
                                                            ↑

Make the reduction to ⟨f⟩ using rule 6a. Goal ⟨f⟩ has now been reached. Remove
⟨f⟩ from the goal stack and resume analysis from step 9′.

    19   1:⟨t⟩;⟨f⟩   ⟨p⟩⟨b⟩   4a⟨t⟩;⟨f⟩
                                                            ↑
Reduce to ⟨n⟩.

    20   1:⟨n⟩   ⟨p⟩⟨b⟩   3⟨n⟩
                                                            ↑

Reduce to ⟨b⟩. Unstack goal ⟨b⟩ and resume analysis from step 3.

    21   1:⟨b⟩   ⟨p⟩   2 1:⟨b⟩
                                                            ↑

Using rule 2 the reduction of 1:⟨b⟩ to ⟨p⟩ is made and we reach the final goal
of the analysis.

In the same way as for bottom up analysis, it is useful to illustrate the
general approach for top down analysis by means of an example. In the grammar
which follows, ⟨sae⟩ should be read as *simple arithmetic expression*, ⟨ae⟩ as
arithmetic expression, ⟨be⟩ as *boolean expression*, and ⟨rel⟩ as *relation*. The
grammar is a simplified extract from the grammar defining Algol 60.

        ⟨ae⟩   ::= ⟨sae⟩ | if ⟨be⟩ then ⟨sae⟩ else ⟨ae⟩

        ⟨sae⟩ ::= a | b | c | d | e

        ⟨rel⟩ ::= ≠ | =

        ⟨be⟩   ::= ⟨sae⟩⟨rel⟩⟨sae⟩

Let us assume that the text to be parsed (analysed) is

    if a = b then c else if a = c then d else e

Using top down analysis we start from the premise that what we have is an ⟨ae⟩.

For this to be true, we must be able to recognise one of the alternatives. Our sub-task is now to recognise ⟨sae⟩ — the first alternative in the definition of ⟨ae⟩ is simply defined as one of the characters a,b,c,d,e. Accordingly the first item in the input stream is examined to determine whether it is one of the five characters listed. In this example it is not, and hence our sub-task of recognising ⟨sae⟩ is abandoned and replaced by the sub-task of identifying the second alternative. Fortunately, a comparison between the input symbol and the first symbol of the second alternative reveals them to be the same and hence our sub-goal is achieved. In order that the analysis can proceed further we shall need to recognise a ⟨be⟩ which now becomes our sub-goal. Recognition of ⟨be⟩ requires first recognition of ⟨sae⟩ and, as a result, the input symbol is compared with each of the five characters which constitute a legitimate ⟨sae⟩. This should be enough to show how top down analysis proceeds. It is also sometimes known as predictive analysis. This name arises since we are forced to select one of the alternatives in a definition to compare it with the input stream. In this sense we are trying to predict the outcome at this stage of the analysis.

We now need to examine more carefully the premises upon which the previous work depends. It must be stated that the methods of analysis outlined will not apply to all grammars. In fact it can be demonstrated that such methods can only be used on a very restricted set of grammars. A formal treatment of grammars here would be lengthy and inappropriate. Much useful material will be found in Gries [1].

In the material on lexical analysis (which in principle is syntax analysis anyway) a finite state recogniser for a floating point constant was used. The rules of the grammar presented were quite restricted in form, consisting of a terminal symbol only or a terminal symbol followed by a non-terminal. (A terminal symbol can be identified in the input stream, a non-terminal will appear in at least one rule on the left hand side). A grammar with rules of this form is a *regular grammar*, or *finite state grammar*, the most restricted of the grammars classified by Chomsky. (See Gries [1] Section 2.10).

Programming languages usually have grammars which are similar to Chomsky type 2. Indeed the fact that a grammar is expressed in BNF implies that it is restricted in this way. But this is no guarantee that such grammars will not cause problems. Consider for example the rule

$$⟨num⟩ ::= ⟨num⟩⟨digit⟩ \mid ⟨digit⟩$$

The first alternative has as its first element the very item being defined. This alternative is thus termed left recursive. Any attempt to use this definition in our top down analysis in the way it has been presented would lead to an infinite loop. Hence our top down methods must assume that there are no rules which have alternatives of this form. Rules using left recursion can be replaced by one or more rules which use right recursion. The following rules also define ⟨num⟩

⟨num⟩ ::= ⟨digit⟩⟨rest of num⟩

⟨rest of num⟩ ::= ⟨digit⟩⟨rest of num⟩ | ⟨null⟩

where by ⟨null⟩ we mean the empty string.

There are many more problems encountered in attempting to produce general parsing methods. Our practical solution, as compiler writers, is to impose restrictions on the grammars we are prepared to deal with, and if necessary rewrite the rules of the grammar so that the same constructions can be generated, whilst being amenable to parsing by the methods we wish to use. Further details of the formal definition of grammar and their suitability for parsing can be found in Gries [1].

How much of the symbol string being parsed are we allowed to examine? In the top down approach as presented, the current input symbol was available for examination, there was no way of looking ahead to the next symbol. However, had it happened that two of the alternatives began with an identical sequence of symbols, then our analysis might encounter an unpredicted input symbol only at the point where they differed. If this happens there is little choice other than to abandon the offending alternative as a prediction, imagine that the input stream has been returned to the state it was at the start of the alternative, and begin afresh on a different alternative. This, for obvious reasons, is known as back tracking and is time consuming. (See slowback and fastback in Rohl [2]). It has also meant that we have had to read several symbols forward in the input stream in order to substantiate or invalidate the prediction.

In contrast, in the example of bottom up analysis the input symbols were kept in a stack, so that the symbols which immediately preceded the current symbol could be easily available for the analysis. Examination of the symbols which surround the current symbol, that is examination of the context in which the current symbol appears, can be extremely helpful in determining the course the analysis should take.

Too much generality can be confusing and in order to offset this it will be helpful to turn attention to the Pascal S compiler. For greater clarity the topic of syntax analysis, like lexical analysis, has been treated as if it were undertaken for the entire user program, without regard to other work which one needs to undertake in compilation. In practice this is unlikely to occur and it never occurs in Pascal S. The *lexical analysis* will be called upon to produce tokens as and when required for analysis, while at suitable points in the analysis a variety of other work will be undertaken. Pascal S undertakes a top down analysis, using a method known as recursive descent. The language is such that a one symbol look ahead is sufficient to enable correct prediction of each syntactic construct.

It is instructive to examine the procedure hierarchy in Pascal S as given in Part 2 together with the syntax diagrams for the language. From these an excellent overview of the compiler organisation is achieved, and should commend the virtues of modular design and construction to the reader. The time required to read and understand the source of the compiler and the accompanying explanatory notes is well spent. Aspects of the analysis undertaken in Pascal S will be highlighted by questions later.

Summary
The purpose of syntax analysis, or parsing, is very simple. It is to establish whether the string of symbols (user program) under consideration is a valid string of symbols according to the grammatical rules of the programming language concerned. In short, could this string have been generated by legitimate application of these rules? If *yes* then the program is valid, if *no* then the program should be rejected. But a user expects more from a compiler than an indication of whether or not a program is syntactically correct. He/she will expect a version of the program which may subsequently be executed to be produced as output by the compiler. Accordingly, attention must be turned to the other tasks which a compiler must undertake.

A note on BNF notation
Special symbols are introduced so that we have a language in which we may talk about a language — the one we are attempting to define. The angle brackets ⟨⟩ enclose *metalinguisitic variables*, the items we are attempting to define. The symbol ::= is read as *is defined as*, and the vertical line is used to separate the alternatives in a definition. Thus

⟨primary colour⟩ ::= red | blue | yellow

⟨rainbow colour⟩ ::= ⟨primary colour⟩ | orange | green |
indigo | violet

This notation BNF was used to define the language Algol 60. It is still frequently used, although various people have at times found it convenient to extend the basic notation given here. The braces {, } are an example of such an extension. A metalinguistic variable is surrounded by braces to indicate that it occurs zero or more times. Such formality is needed to allow the writer to define what he means for the reader, without having to rely on assumptions which may have much in common but which may not be identical.

EXERCISES

1. Examine the rules of the grammar given below:—

i)	S ::= aSBC	iv)	bB ::= bb
ii)	S ::= abC	v)	bC ::= bc
iii)	CB ::= BC	vi)	cC ::= cc

Starting with S, the *distinguished* symbol, demonstrate how the strings abc, aaabbbccc, are derived. Show, informally, that the strings abbc, aabc, abcc, cannot be derived from the above rules.

2. Use the bottom up method outlined in the text to parse the following string

    begin d; s; 1 :begin d; d; s; s end end .

3. Express the syntax for VARIABLE, given in the Pascal S syntax diagrams, in BNF notation.

4. Does the procedure IFSTATEMENT in the Pascal S compiler correctly parse an if statement as defined in the syntax diagrams? If not say why not.

5. In the program ERRORS below, the error numbers produced by Pascal S have been omitted. By considering the program and the Pascal S listing, fill in the error numbers which should follow the ↑ symbol. (The only numbers used are given under KEY WORDS in the listing).

```
      0   program errors(output);
      0
      0   const      space=' ';
      0              upper='a';
      0              finish=false;
      0              message='finished';
****                         ↑
      0              lower='u';
      0
      0   type    nametype=array[1 .. 10] of char;
      0           listype  =array[lower .. upper] of nametype;
****                                        ↑
      0
      0   var     str:string;
****                    ↑
      0           i, j : integer;
      0           list : listype;
      0           quit : boolean;
      0
      0   procedure setup(var 1:1istype,bot,top:char);
****                          ↑
      0   var     blankstrng:nametype;
      0           i:interger;
****                 ↑
```

```
   0   begin
   0     for i:=1 to 10 do blankstring:=space;
****                  ↑      ↑           ↑    - - - -
   5   for i:=bot to top do 1:blankstring;
****                ↑    ↑            ↑
  12   end; (* setup *)
  12
  12   begin
  13     setup(list,lower, upper);
  18     writeline('do you wish to continue ?');
****            ↑ - - - - - - - - - - - - - - - - - -
  18     read(str);
****        ↑
  20     quit:=if str='y' then true else false;
****            ↑              ↑       ↑     ↑
  25
  25   (* etc etc *)
  25
  25   end.
```
compiled with errors

key words
```
 0    undef id
14    ;
19    type
20    prog.param
27    indexbound
35    types
45    var, proc
50    constant
58    factor
```

Chapter 3

Symbol Tables – Structure and Access

One of the benefits to the user of using an assembly language or a high level programming language is the ability to use symbols to represent the data items he wishes to manipulate. It follows then that all language processors for languages offering these facilities must have provision for dealing with user symbols. This is necessary in order to ensure that user symbols are used in a logical and consistent fashion. Thus, all language processors will use a table to record such details of a user symbol as are considered necessary. Entering symbols into such a symbol table and their subsequent recognition can be time consuming, and as a result some discussion of different methods which might be used is required.

It should be stated at the outset that the amount and type of information stored with each symbol varies from compiler to compiler and from assembler to assembler. At the very least a given number of characters from the character string which is the symbol will be stored and, in the case of a compiler, the type associated with the symbol will also be stored. In most block structured high level languages, all user symbols must be explicitly defined in a suitable declaration. However, it is well to remember that, in Fortran for example, different conventions for typing are used. By default, a user symbol is typed as integer if the first letter of the symbol is one of I, J, K, L, M, or N. A symbol starting with any other letter is typed as real. Many Fortran programs contain no declarative statements because of this default convention. Let us assume that the language being processed requires a declaration to be made, so that it may be assumed that symbol names are entered into the symbol table while processing a declaration. The simplest approach to adopt is to enter names into the table as they are encountered. When processing the statements which follow the declarations, the occurrence of a user symbol will cause us to ascertain whether this symbol exists in the table. The simplest way to do this is to start at the head of the table and examine each item in turn. If a match or hit is made then the symbol has been defined; if the end of the table is reached without locating the symbol, then the symbol has not been declared. This method is easy to understand and program but not very efficient. It is right that some consideration be given to efficiency because access to the table must be made for every occurrence of each user symbol. If the symbol table has n entries then, for the scheme above, on average half the entries in the table must be examined before the required entry is located. Thus, it is said that the *search length* is $n/2$. When there are a large number of entries in the table, $n/2$ is unacceptably large. This search method is known as a linear search and it is easy to do better than this.

For a large table, some way of restricting the area of the table to be searched would be most helpful, so that even in the worst case we would not have to search half the table. What is frequently done in practice for example with library catalogue cards, is to order them alphabetically by author. Then a search is restricted to those entries which start with the letter of interest and the area of search is considerably reduced. In order that this approach can be realised in a program, two tables would be needed. One would give for each letter of the alphabet the first entry in the symbol table where symbols starting with this symbol were stored. The other table would be the symbol table. This is shown diagramatically in Figure 3.1.

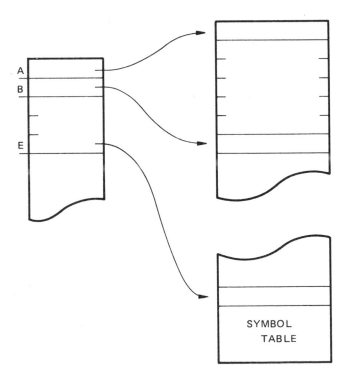

Fig. 3.1 — Alphabetic indexing into a symbol table.

If we assume that items were entered into the appropriate area of the symbol table as they were encountered, then the entries in the different alphabetic groups would not be ordered as they are in a library catalogue. Nonetheless, our search now becomes one of locating the start of entries for a particular letter of the alphabet, followed by a linear search of the appropriate area of the symbol table. The efficiency of our search will now depend upon the way symbols are distributed amongst the possible starting letters. In many cases this will make this search more efficient than the simple linear search, although clearly in the pathological case where all user symbols started with the same letter, the difference between the two schemes will be small. The objection to the method as given, is its assumption of predefined areas of the table for each letter. If these areas are too large we waste space. If they are too small the method breaks down.

If the notion of ordering the symbols in the symbol table is taken further, the search can be made more efficient. It is usually straightforward to compare two symbols and say that one is less, equal, or greater than the other. If the entries in a symbol table are arranged in ascending (or descending) order the search length can be considerably reduced. Considering the whole table initially, we ask if the symbol to be located is less than or greater than the symbol in the middle of the table. (If it is equal to the middle symbol our search is complete!). If it is less than the symbol in the middle of the table, then, since the table is ordered, we ignore the top half and consider the bottom half of the table. Equally, if our symbol is greater than the middle entry of the table, the top half of the table only need be considered. The process of constantly halving the size of the table is repeated until our symbol is, or is not, located. This method, known as the logarithmic search, or binary chop, is more efficient than the two forms of searching previously described, but has the disadvantage of requiring the elements of the symbol table to be ordered. A logarithmic search will usually not be realistic for user defined symbols, since we must either gather all symbols and then sort them, which would be time consuming, or we must insert a symbol into the table in such a way as to preserve its ordering. This would mean moving existing entries to make way for the new entry and would significantly increase the time taken to make a new entry into the table.

A tree structure was earlier used to illustrate the terms top down and bottom up in discussing syntax analysis. A tree structure is also a convenient one in which to store user symbols. The first user symbol, say count, is termed the root if it is the first entry in the structure. Succeeding symbols will be compared first with count, then with all other symbols stored in the tree structure. The tree will be created by branching left at any node when the current symbol is less than the node symbol, and branching right if the current symbol is greater than the node symbol. Thus the occurrence of the identifiers max, min, mark, best, following count would lead to the structure given diagramatically in Figure 3.2.

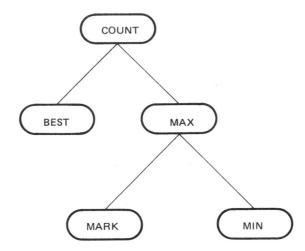

Fig. 3.2 — Part of a tree structured symbol table.
Note that if the identifiers were entered in a different order a different tree would result.

Clearly following each comparison, the portion of the symbol table to be searched is significantly reduced, and thus this method is superior to the linear search. However, only if the tree were symmetric would the area of table to be searched be halved each time. Hence results will not be as good as those achieved with binary chop, but the advantage here is that this tree structure can be used for user symbols.

A popular technique over many years for symbol table organization has been the hashing technique. Once again the idea behind this approach is to reduce the area of table to be searched. In this case it is achieved by *processing* the user symbol in such a way as to produce a numeric result. This result will ideally be the entry point of the user symbol in the symbol table. The transition from user symbol (which is a string of characters) to numeric result is achieved by a hashing function. This function may form the weighted sum of the ordinal values of the characters of the symbol or it may simply sum the ordinal values of the characters (which does not produce a good hash); alternatively, it may manipulate all or part of the bit pattern of the internal representation of the symbol. The possibilities are enormous and are only limited by the imagination of the constructor. However, of the many theoretical possibilities available, few will prove economic and efficient in practice. Ideally of course a hashing function would produce a unique number (entry) for every user symbol. If this happens then the user symbol is located at the first comparison. More usually several symbols will map onto one entry position, and so this possibility must be catered for. A straightforward way of dealing with this is to add to the hash value (hv) a suitably chosen increment (i) and compute ($hv + i$) $\underline{\text{mod}}$ m where

m is the table size. This is simply moving on from the start position by adding an increment to form a new hash value. This process is repeated until a hit is obtained. In order that this process can visit all entries in the table, i, m need to be co-prime (i.e. they have no factors in common) otherwise it would be possible to visit repeatedly the same elements in the table. As in the choice of hashing function, a great variety of ways is available for *rehashing*, that is, deciding how to select the next element of the symbol table when the original hash function maps two symbols onto one entry. The size of a hash table can be critical in its efficiency; it should not be allowed to get too full, because in this situation one must rehash more frequently, thus losing efficiency. It is therefore recommended that m, the size of the hash table as used above, should be chosen so that the table is half as big again as the expected number of symbols.

Clearly a wide variety of methods and techniques exist for the construction of and access to symbol tables. This is because such tables are heavily used at compile time and therefore it is important to give due consideration to efficiency. But efficiency involves consideration of space as well as speed, and it might well be that an implementor would rather have a slower method which was economical in space, rather than fast access hashing method which required considerable table space. The implementor must make this choice.

In considering table access and structure in general, no comment has been made about the effect of block structure on our symbol tables. Any block structured language allows its users to define the same symbol name in different blocks, and in particular it can be redeclared from block to block so that it may be of integer type in one block and of boolean type in another. A symbol used in this way may have more than one entry in the symbol table at the same time. No confusion should exist between the two symbols. As may perhaps be expected, there is more than one method of resolving this satisfactorily. Most methods involve the use of static block level, or the lexical level at which a block is encountered. Remember that an identifier may be used in the block in which it is declared or any lexicographically enclosed block. The block number (which is unique) is obtained by incrementing a counter for every block encountered, while the block level (which is not unique) is obtained by incrementing a counter at the start of every block and decrementing it at the end of every block. Only when exit is made from the block in which an identifier is declared is an identifier inaccessible. If we are using hashing techniques for our symbol table, then one method of forcing a distinction between identical identifiers declared in different blocks is to incorporate the block number at which the identifier is declared into the symbol name before hashing. This would certainly assure different entries into the symbol table for symbols with the same name. Perhaps more usually a symbol table will be organised so that all the entries at any level are chained together. This will require additionally that a table of the position of the first identifier at a particular level in the symbol table is kept (DISPLAY in Pascal S). A search for the entry for any particular symbol must now be rather differently organised. First the entries at the current level are searched, if no match is found, then a search of the previous level (the block which encloses the current block) is made. This search of preceding levels is continued until the symbol is found, or until all accessible identifiers have been checked. A table organised in this way offers the additional economy that, when the end of a block is reached, all the symbol table space associated with identifiers declared in that block can be released for re-use. Note that this is not done in Pascal S, since the full symbol table must be preserved for use in the run time environment.

Finally, something needs to be said of the contents of the symbol table we are to use. Clearly we must store the string of characters which constitute the symbol name. In addition we may expect to store its type, and what we might call its mode, that is whether it is a constant or a variable, or perhaps whether it is a procedure or a function. This information will help to determine that the symbol is used in the appropriate way and that its type is correct in the context in which it is used. For arrays and other more complex structures, we must be able to hold additional information about the index range, the type of index, the type of element etc. In short the symbol table must hold such information as to permit a wide range of semantic checks at compile time to enable the generation of a lower level version of the source program of maximum integrity. To achieve this the symbol table must also hold either the run time address of the symbol concerned or sufficient information for this to be computed later. This, however, assumes familiarity with the run time environment, and this is discussed later.

The symbol table in Pascal S, called TAB, is arranged so that user symbols encountered in compilation are all stored and none discarded. The array DISPLAY is used as a stack. Its indices indicate the lexical level, while its contents point to the first user symbol in TAB at that level. ATAB holds in each entry sufficient information to define a vector. Thus, when TAB holds an array name, it will also hold for the array name a reference to ATAB the array table. In Pascal each block is necessarily uniquely associated with a procedure or function. Since this means that more information needs to be held than is accommodated in TAB, an additional table BTAB is used. BTAB finds an additional use in holding information about the records permitted in Pascal S. On its declaration each record is treated like a block and hence BTAB is used as an additional store.

Full details of the contents of the various tables used in Pascal S and the relationships between the tables are given in Part 2.

Further illustrations of the variety in construction and of contents in symbol tables can be found in Gries [1].

EXERCISES

1. The program skeleton given is taken from an article by Sale [13], and is to test the scope rules of Pascal. Will Pascal S flag any errors in connection with <u>state</u>?

> <u>program</u> nonstandard(output);
> <u>type</u>   state = <u>record</u>
>   status : (defined, undefined);
>   value   : integer
>   <u>end</u>;
>
> <u>procedure</u> innerscope;
>   <u>var</u>   ageofperson : state;
>   state : (scanning, found, notpresent);
>   <u>begin</u>
>   (* including references to variable state *)
>   <u>end</u>;
>
> <u>begin</u>
>   (* program body *)
> <u>end</u>.

2. A hashing function given by Rohl [2] is

$$C_1*2^{n-1} + C_2*2^{n-2} + \ldots + C_n \; ,$$

(where the integer corresponding to the ith character of an n character identifier is referred to as C_i).
Select six identifiers and compute their hash value and their hash value mod 10.

3. Reconstruct the identifier declarations from the symbol table, produced by Pascal S, which is given here.

identifiers	link	obj	typ	ref	nrm	lev	adr
28	27	3	0	2	1	0	125
29 hours	0	4	2	3	1	1	47
30 t1	0	1	1	0	1	2	5
31 t2	30	1	1	0	1	2	6
32 t3	31	1	1	0	1	2	7
33 t4	32	1	1	0	1	2	8
34 valid	33	1	3	0	1	2	9
35 reasonable	34	1	3	0	1	2	10
36 lapse	35	4	2	4	1	2	0

37 ta	0	1	1	0	1	3	5
38 tb	37	1	1	0	1	3	6
39 ha	38	1	1	0	1	3	7
40 ma	39	1	1	0	1	3	8
41 hb	40	1	1	0	1	3	9
42 mb	41	1	1	0	1	3	10
43 rest	42	1	2	0	1	3	11

blocks	last	1par	psze	vsze
1	28	1	0	0
2	29	28	5	5
3	36	33	9	11
4	43	38	7	12

4. List the procedures and functions provided as standard by Pascal S. What happens if a user program defines, say, a procedure, having the same name as one of the items in your list? Give reasons for your answer.

5. In the procedure INSYMBOL a binary search is used to find 'id' in 'key'. Assume that 'id' takes as starting value the value of an element in 'key', and determine how many comparisons are required before the correct element is located. Repeat this for each element of 'key'.

Chapter 4

The Run Time Environment

In the preceding chapters we have considered how the source program submitted by the user may be processed. This processing has caused us to be able to recognise symbols within the program and hence the larger constructs of the language. However, the user ultimately requires a version of his high level language program which will execute on one or more machines. This means that a low level version of the source program must be generated. Before this can sensibly be done, the way in which the data objects, which the user's program seeks to manipulate, are stored and processed must be carefully considered and well defined. In short, the environment within which operations are carried out at run time must be planned in order that sensible and logical instructions may be generated at compile time. In particular this will mean that provision must be made for storing, and referring to, all the data objects defined in the user program.

Of the high level languages, Fortran has one of the simplest schemes for storage management and access. Accordingly, a brief look at such a scheme is useful to set the scene. A simple Fortran program consists of one or more program units which are disjoint and textually separated. There must be a main program, all other program units are subroutines or functions, with the exception of the BLOCK DATA unit which can be ignored for the purposes of this discussion. If the same name is used in different units it is treated as a separate entity in each unit. No recursion is allowed, and the upper and lower bounds of arrays must be explicitly stated at compile time. These factors mean that, for data objects defined in one unit, a storage area of known size and organisation can be determined at compile time. Thus the one or more storage elements required by any data object can be allocated. This may be done by giving explicit memory addresses (absolute addressing) or by considering the address of each data object relative to the start of the data storage area.

The allocation of storage to an identifier will be done either when its definition is encountered or, in Fortran, when the identifier is defined by virtue of its use. In the Figure 4.1 it may be assumed for example that I, J, K are integers requiring one storage unit, R is a real requiring two storage units whilst N is an array (a dimensioned variable) requiring six storage units. The offset into the data area for any symbol will be held in the symbol table.

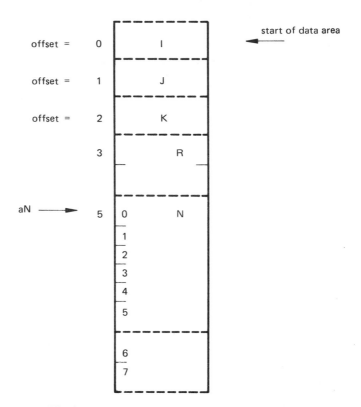

Fig. 4.1 – An arrangement of I, J, K. R, N in store.

It is easy to see how access is made to individual items in the example presented. It is perhaps not quite so easy to see how access is made to the dimensioned variable N since no mention has been made of how N is defined. Let us consider three possible definitions for N.

   i) DIMENSION N(8)

   ii) DIMENSION N(4, 2)

   iii) DIMENSION N(2, 2, 2)

Assume that in all three cases the elements of N require one storage unit. Allocating the storage area to N upon encountering one of the definitions above causes no problems. What we must also be able to do is to refer satisfactorily to the correct part of the data storage area for each of the references N(I), N(I, J), N(I, J, K) corresponding to the examples above. If we write aN for the address of N then the reference N(I) means computing

$$aN + I - 1$$

to refer to the appropriate element of N. As soon as the number of dimensions exceeds one, more care is needed in our computation, as shown in Figure 4.2.

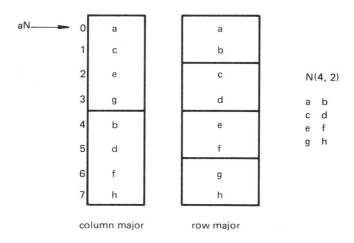

Fig. 4.2 – Storing the elements of a two dimensional array.

We note that the second definition of the array N could lead us to consider it being stored as four elements twice or as two elements four times. The first is known as column major order (considering the usual array interpretation that N is four rows of two columns) where the elements of columns are stored consecutively. The second is known as row major order where the elements of rows are stored consecutively. While it makes little or no difference to the access mechanism, many Fortran implementations use column major order whilst many Algol-like languages use row major order. In either situation one needs to arrange an expression which will use one subscript to hop over the rows/ columns of no interest, leaving the second subscript to provide an appropriate offset on the required row or column. Thus the reference N(I, J) will mean computing

for column major order $aN + (J-1) * 4 + (I-1)$

check .. for I=1, J=1 –>   aN

I=4, J=2 –> $aN + 1 * 4 + 3$

for row major order $aN + (I-1) * 2 + (J-1)$

$I=1, J=1 \rightarrow$ aN

$I=4, J=2 \rightarrow$ $aN + 3 * 2 + 1$

If the number of elements in each dimension remains as above, but we represent the lower bound of the dimensions by 1bI, 1bJ, then the expressions become

for column major order $aN + (J-1bJ) * 4 + (I-1bI)$

for row major order $aN + (I-1bI) * 2 + (J-1bJ)$.

To lead us more easily into further generality, let us consider the three dimensional case with the reference N(I, J, K), and let us simply consider the case of row major order so that we have

$$aN + (I-1bI) * 2 * 2 + (J-1bJ) * 2 + (K-1bK)$$

and when the lower bounds are all 1

$I=1, J=1, K=1 \rightarrow aN$

$I=2, J=2, K=2 \rightarrow aN + 2 + 2 + 1$

Finally, denoting the upper bound of a dimension by 'ub' we calculate the number of elements in, say, the dimension referenced by I as

$$ubI - 1bI + 1$$

which can be called the *stride* of this dimension. Access to the three dimensional array N is thus achieved by

$$aN + (I-1bI)*strideJ*strideK + (J-1bJ)*strideK + (K-1bK)$$

Note that the expression can conveniently be rearranged to give a constant part, which can thus be evaluated at compile time, and a variable part which can only be computed when the values of I, J, K are known. If the lower bound of all dimensions is one, then the expression becomes

$$aN + (I-1) * ubJ * ubK + (J-1) * ubK + (K-1)$$

where ub is written for upper bound.

The corresponding expression for an array with any number of dimensions can be imagined. Once again this expression can be rearranged to give a constant part and a variable part. Only the variable part would be evaluated at run time. In terms of efficiency a multiply operation can be relatively slow, so it is worth noting that some array access schemes have used one subscript to access a table which gives the position in data storage dictated by that subscript's contribution.

(See Gries [1] Chapter 8). However increase in speed is bought by increase in the space required by the additional table. Before leaving this topic some comment must be made about error checking. The message *subscript out of range* is one that many programmers are familiar with and it should be noted that crude subscript checks are easy but worthless. In the case of the expressions generated previously for access, it is easy to check that the part of the expression following aN gives a non-negative value less than 8. However, that will not help the programmer who is unfortunate enough to generate the reference N(1, 3, 2) which will produce aN + 0 + 4 + 1 if evaluated by our example. The reference is invalid but the check suggested will not identify it as invalid. The check suggested is not a subscript check but an *address out of range* check. The only sound procedure to adopt is to check that each subscript is valid within the range prescribed for it.

The preceding details, whilst relevant to Fortran, will serve us well in examining more complex and useful storage strategies required by block structured languages. A key feature in these schemes will be the stack, a data structure that has already received mention but which will be further examined in the following paragraphs.

In outlining in simple terms the role of an identifier in Fortran, the term unit was used to denote the different program portions in which an identifier might be defined and used. In Algol 60 the term block was used to denote the portion of user program in which an identifier is defined and used. A program was a rather special block and contained all other blocks which could if necessary be nested. In Algol 60 a procedure or function body was a block, but a block was not necessarily the body of a procedure or function, hence, a program could contain many blocks but no procedures or functions. In Pascal, which like Algol 60, Algol 68 and others is considered a block structured language, the term block is used quite specifically to cover the declarations of executable statements of a program, a procedure or a function. As a result there is a one-to-one relationship between the number of procedures or functions declared in a program and the number of blocks the program contains. In the following part of the text we shall use block in the sense it is used in the definition of Pascal.

Each block may contain the definition of various items. Such items are said to be local to the block. They are local variables. But since blocks may be nested, i.e. one declared within another, identifiers declared in an outer block are, unless re-defined, available for use in an inner block. Such items are said to be global to the block. Thus in any block, a user may use not only identifiers declared in that block but identifiers declared in any or all of the blocks which enclose that block. Thus we may have to generate references not only to the data store of the block whose statements we are processing, but also to the data store of enclosing blocks. Each call of a procedure (which means entering a new block) requires that the storage space associated with that procedure becomes available for use. But in block structured languages a procedure is allowed to call itself. This second call of the procedure must also require that the storage space associated with the procedure becomes available to use. Clearly if the second call of the procedure used the same storage area as the first, then when this second call is complete and we attempt to complete the first call, it would be foolish to assume that the data storage area is still as it was prior to the second call. In order to ensure that one call of a procedure does not corrupt the data storage area assumed by a prior and uncompleted call, each call of a procedure results in a new data storage area being used for the local variables. The allocation and deallocation of storage in this manner is most easily accomplished on a stack, as shown in Figure 4.3.

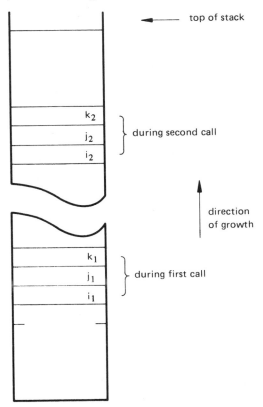

Fig. 4.3 – Each procedure call creates a new stack frame.

Thus, in the diagram, when the first call of a procedure in which i, j, k are defined is made, they will have positions i_1, j_1, k_1. If this first call of the procedure results in a second call then i, j, k will now refer to the positions i_2, j_2, k_2. Upon exit from a procedure the local variable space is no longer required. Accordingly after exit from the second call of the procedure i, j, k once more refer to

i_1, j_1, k_1 which have thus retained their values during the second call, since they were inaccesible for the duration of that call.

Thus while in the Fortran example the identifiers I, J, K were allocated storage as an offset from the start of a single data area, in the present example the identifiers are allocated storage as an offset from an element of the stack. This element may well be different from one call of the procedure to the next. The Fortran scheme has the advantage of simplicity without much flexibility, whereas the stack storage scheme offers the advantages that it allows recursion, and saves space, because the storage area for local variables of any procedure only occupies space on the stack when the procedure is active. The only disadvantage is the amount of overhead necessary to administer the stack storage scheme. This overhead is usually small but its size will of course depend upon the architecture of the underlying machine.

There is no difficulty in envisaging how this scheme deals with arrays in Pascal since, as in Fortran, the size of the array can be determined at compile time. Accordingly the accessing mechanism is as before except that it is relative to a stack position rather than to a fixed data area. Storage of Pascal S records on a stack causes no problems. Given the record definition it is simply necessary to compute the size of all fields and compute references to fields in much the same way as for arrays. For records with variant parts the *worst case* size is computed. Items such as strings can be more of a nuisance because they are more convenient to the user as items having no fixed length. However, in the run time environment it is much more acceptable to know the lengths of the items which must be stored and manipulated. Thus one solution is to precede each string by an indicator saying how many characters are in the string. This will be quite transparent to the user but advantageous to the compiler writer, because it means that two other possibilities, either of computing the length of a string, or of assuming a fixed but large upper limit on the number of characters it contains, need not be considered.

The idea of associating with an item at run time such information as will help its manipulation is not confined to strings. One feature of Algol 60 which its users found to be missing in early versions of Pascal is the dynamic array, that is an array for which the bounds are determined at run time rather than at compile time. (This omission is rectified in the ISO standard for Pascal [11] by the introduction of conformant array parameters. An array which is a parameter to a procedure or function can include its type definition in the parameter list and the bounds can be variable identifiers).

Consider the statements below

        read (input, limita, limitb)

        . . . .

        N: array [1 . . limita, 1 . . limitb] of integer

This could not form part of a Pascal program but perhaps illustrates the principle, namely that at compile time the size of N could not be determined as it was for our earlier examples. Rather, the size of N can only be determined when the values of limita, limitb have been read, that is when the program is being executed. This situation can be dealt with by forming a table or vector of information concerning the array N at compile time. Such information as is available at compile time is stored in the vector and the remaining information is stored in the vector as and when it becomes available at run time. The object of the exercise is to ensure that, by the time a reference to an array element is encountered, all relevant information to enable computation of the reference, such as we have already seen, is available. This is done successfully in many compilers, but it is not necessary for implementations of Pascal in which arrays with dynamic bounds are not allowed. For further information on the form and content of the 'dope vector' see Gries [1] chapter 8.

4.1 PROCEDURE ENTRY, PROCEDURE EXIT

In the preceding description of storage on a run time stack and reference to items in this storage, it was made clear that procedure entry and exit dictated the creation and deletion of stack frames. Thus the instructions needed to do this must be generated at these points. Control and organisation of stack frames is easily and economically achieved in at least two ways. Before detailing these two methods let us recall that only procedures which are currently active have storage space on the stack and that, within any procedure, reference may be made to global variables. Such global variables must exist in blocks which enclose the block in which they are used. Hence a link to such blocks must be preserved. This will be called a static link because it can be determined by considering the relationship of the various blocks as given in the program listing. At run time the static link will point from, say, the current stack <u>frame</u> (the area of stack associated with a procedure) to the base of the stack frame of the lexicographically enclosing block. This frame in turn will point to the frame for its enclosing block. Thus by following this chain backwards, the frame in which the required global variables may be accessed is determined. Since a procedure may call itself and, in so doing, create new stack frames, each of these stack frames must also point back to the base of its predecessor. Then, when upon procedure exit a frame is released, the base of the previous (calling) frame is easily recovered. This link will be called the dynamic link.

The static link, while necessary, can if implemented as described above, impose an overhead on variable access. It should be clear that if in compilation a count is incremented for each block entered and decremented for each block exit, the result is a level number for each block. By obtaining for each global variable reference a level difference, that being the difference in levels between the level at which it is used and the level at which it is declared, access to a variable is easily given as a level difference plus an offset. Thus, at run time, access is gained by following the static link down through the number of frames specified by the level difference, and then using the offset in the last frame. This form of access is used by the Pascal P system (Daniels [10], Barron [9]).

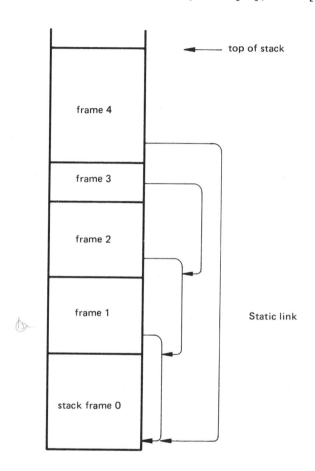

Fig. 4.4 — The static link refers to the stack frame of the enclosing block.

program slink(output);

(* this program skeleton illustrates how the static links assumed by Figure 4.4 might arise *)

procedure a;
begin
end; (* a *)

```
procedure b;

  procedure c;

    procedure d;
    begin
        a;   (* link snapshot following call of a *)
    end; (* d *)

  begin
    d;
  end; (* c *)

begin
  c;
end; (* b *)

begin (* program body*)
  b;
end.
```

Pascal S adopts a different strategy. The static links and dynamic links as described are calculated and are stored on the stack. In addition the array DISPLAY is used, and its function is to provide pointers to the currently accessible stack frames. This is achieved by using the level number, as described earlier for a procedure, as the index into DISPLAY. If now a variable is described by the level number (rather than difference) and an offset, then it may be referenced by using the level number to extract from DISPLAY the base of the stack frame and the offset may be used as before. This method achieves more rapid access to variables, because a chain does not have to be followed, but attracts the additional overhead that DISPLAY must be kept up to date.

We have seen that a stack frame is used to hold local variables and housekeeping information such as the links just described. It must also be used to hold information concerning procedure parameters. Procedure parameters in Pascal are limited, and are further restricted in Pascal S so that a procedure or function name may not be a parameter. Thus in comparison with, say Algol 68, what is described here is rather a simple scheme. A parameter may have one of two modes, either a value parameter or a var parameter. With value parameters the user is expected to provide as a parameter simply an item whose value is used by the procedure; this could, for example, be an expression, or a function call. A procedure cannot change an actual parameter which is a variable when the corresponding formal parameter is a value parameter. This is because, for value parameters, space is allocated in the stack frame for an item of size appropriate for the parameter. On procedure entry the value of the actual parameter is copied into this local space and it is this local item (not the original) which is used, and possibly changed. Those parameters preceded by the word <u>var</u> may be changed by the procedure and accordingly it is the address of these parameters which is stored locally in the stack frame. Thus when any reference to this parameter is made, it is the *original* which is used and may be changed.

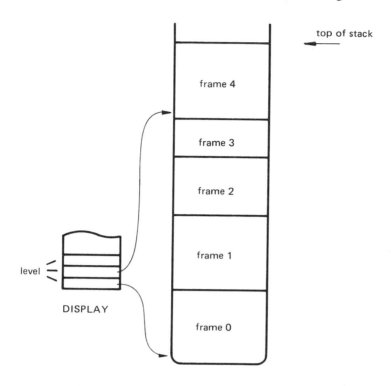

Fig. 4.5 — DISPLAY points to the currently active frames at each static level.

It has been necessary to describe certain aspects of the run time environment in some detail, since this has a considerable influence upon the instructions generated by the compiler to ensure successful execution of the user program. The storage arrangements so far considered have been those undertaken by the compiler for the data objects defined by the user. Apart from defining these objects the user has exercised no control over the storage arrangements. If the user is allowed some control, then it is likely that he can use memory more economically than he otherwise would. For example Fortran allows the user to define a COMMON area. This is an area of memory which may be used by any program unit which requests access. In this way memory can be shared by program units which are otherwise independent of each other. A COMMON area usually has a name associated with it and a Fortran program may have many COMMON areas though it need not have any. Use of COMMON enables the user to control which program units share data, and since the number of COMMON areas and their size is known at compile time, it may be called user-controlled static storage. A program is much more useful if the language in which it is written allows the user some control over storage organisation. In particular a program which can request more memory as and when required is more useful than one which obtains more memory only as a result of a program change and subsequent re-compilation. Pascal P, the *portable* Pascal, offers the user limited dynamic control of memory at run time. A user-controlled stack is provided and a user is able to *record* the level of his stack by issuing a MARK instruction. After making requests for memory space using the NEW instruction the user may issue further MARK instructions. Each MARK instruction has a pointer as a parameter. The user retains this as a position indicator. RELEASE, which also takes a pointer as a parameter, will free the dynamically controlled memory from the present position to the pointer given as parameter. Data objects can only be freed in the order they were obtained and this is inconvenient in many applications. The ISO Standard Pascal offers the user NEW to obtain memory for a data object and DISPOSE to free the memory associated with a data object. A pointer must be provided as parameter to each procedure. Algol 68 offers more ambitious dynamic storage still in the form of a heap on which objects and subvalues of any mode and length may be stored. The heap is used to store objects such as strings (an array of characters which has dynamic bounds) which vary in size through the execution of the program. Use of such data objects requires memory to be repeatedly allocated and freed, and causes fragmentation of the free memory in the storage area. An automatic garbage collection system is required to recognise and collect together unused fragments of memory. This process may be complex and time consuming (see Knuth [4]). A wide variety of storage control facilities can be made available to the high level language user and not all have been mentioned here. The language designer must decide on the facilities which seem most appropriate for the intended users of the language.

In discussing the run time environment, attention has focused on storage requirements of the user's program. It would also be legitimate to consider what use the user's program might make at run time of the hardware facilities of the host machine. However since the later work on code generation concerns Pascal S, which is portable and machine independent, specific machine facilities will not be considered.

EXERCISES

1. On many computers a floating point number will occupy twice as many storage elements (words, bytes) as an integer. Assume this is the case for the machine on which the Pascal S program executes, and calculate how much memory the run time stack 's' occupies.

2. Is a satisfactory check made at run time on the values of array subscripts processed by the Pascal S interpreter?

3. Determine the maximum depth of recursion which could be achieved by a user procedure (or function) running under the version of Pascal S which is listed.

4. Is the 'updatedisplay' instruction generated at the exit from every procedure (or function)? Give reasons to support your answer.

5. In the example below various values are missing from the stack snapshots. By careful consideration of the information given identify the missing values.

```
 0  program stack(output);
 0
 0  (*$t+, s+*)
 0
 0  type    intarr = array [1 .. 4] of integer;
 0
 0
 0  var     m,n : integer;
 0              r : real;
 0              a : intarr;
 0
 0  procedure setup(ns:integer; check:real);
 0  var        k, 1 : integer;
 0
 0  function total (var at:intarr; nt:integer):integer;
 0  var    i, sum : integer;
 0  begin
 0
 0  for i:=1 to nt do sum:=sum+at [i] ;
13  total:=sum;
16
16  end; (* total *)
16
16  begin
17
17  1:=27+total(a,ns);
25
25  end; (* setup *)
25
25  begin
26      n:=4; setup(n,5.75);
33  end .
```

identifiers	link	obj	typ	ref	nrm	lev	adr
28	27	3	0	2	1	0	26
29 intarr	0	2	5	1	0	1	4
30 m	29	1	1	0	1	1	5
31 n	30	1	1	0	1	1	6
32 r	31	1	2	0	1	1	7
33 a	32	1	5	1	1	1	8
34 set up	33	3	0	3	1	1	17
35 ns	0	1	1	0	1	2	5
36 check	35	1	2	0	1	2	6
37 k	36	1	1	0	1	2	7
38 l	37	1	1	0	1	2	8
39 total	38	4	1	4	1	2	0
40 at	0	1	5	1	0	3	5
41 nt	40	1	1	0	1	3	6
42 i	41	1	1	0	1	3	7
43 sum	42	1	1	0	1	3	8

blocks	last	1par	psze	vsze
1	28	1	0	0
2	34	28	5	12
3	39	36	7	9
4	43	41	7	9

arrays	xtyp	etyp	eref	low	high	elsz	size
1	1	1	0	1	4	1	4

code:

```
 0     0 3      7,
 1     24       1,
 2      1 3     6,
 3     14      13
 4      0 3     8,
 5      1 3     8,
 6      1 3     5,
 7      1 3     7,
 8     20       1,
 9     34        ,
10     52        ,
11     38        ,
12     15       4,
13      0 3     0,
14      1 3     8,
```

15	38	,
16	33	,
17	0 2	8,
18	24	27,
19	18	39,
20	0 1	8,
21	1 2	5,
22	19	6,
23	52	,
24	38	,
25	32	,
26	0 1	6,
27	24	4,
28	38	,
29	18	34,
30	1 1	6,
31	25	1,
32	19	6,
33	31	,

Starting address is   26

calling setup
level 1
start of code 17

contents of display

| 1 | 0 |
| 0 | 0 |

top of stack   20   frame base   12

stack contents

20	0
19	0
18	16568
17	4
16	34
15	0
14	0
13	33
12	6
11	0
10	0

9	0
8	0
7	0
6	4
5	0
4	28
3	−1
2	0
1	0

⟨ = = =⟩

calling	total
level	2
start of code	0

contents of display

2	12
1	0
0	0

top of stack   31   frame base   23

stack contents

31	0
30	0
29	
28	
27	
26	
25	
24	
23	0
22	27
21	20
20	0
19	0
18	16568
17	4
16	34
15	0
14	0
13	33
12	6

11	0
10	0
9	0
8	0
7	0
6	4
5	0
4	28
3	−1
2	0
1	0

⟨ = = = ⟩

.

Chapter 5
Semantic Processing

We have considered such matters as the organisation and operation of the symbol table, and the means of controlling the run time stack in isolation from the rest of the compilation process. They are however vital to this process and therefore must be integrated with the syntax analysis already discussed. This integration may be done in different ways and is briefly considered below.

The reading, by a program, of the user's source program or a reduced version of it, may be called a *pass*. Usually more processing than simply reading is associated with a pass, and the word is thought to derive from the time when a card deck had to be inserted into a reader and read more than once. Hence, one reads or hears of one pass compilers, two pass assemblers and so on. The number of passes needed to compile a program will be unknown to the modern user with files on disk, since intermediate versions of his program will be written and read from filestore. However, in considering the compilation process it is of interest to know whether a one pass or, say, a nine pass system is more desirable. There is no easy answer. Using several passes will clearly mean a significant increase in the input/output processing required by the compiler, but it provides more opportunity to refine and optimise the code version of the original source which is produced. A single pass compiler has less input/output traffic and less scope for producing *good code*. More pertinently perhaps, splitting the work of a compiler into several passes can be extremely helpful in focussing attention on the processing required in any particular pass. It may not be done in any practical implementation, but one can imagine each of the processes so far discussed, lexical analysis, syntax analysis, as each occupying one pass. More usually no such clear cut distinction can be made. Pascal compilers were conceived as one pass systems. The design of the language helps significantly in this (as it was intended to do). Recall that in discussing top down analysis we saw that it would frequently be necessary to try several alternatives before obtaining the correct one. If in recognising a particular language construct we may, at the same time, be generating code to realise this construct at a low level, then the discovery that we have been following the wrong alternative also means that we have generated unwanted code. Accordingly we must try to ensure that this does not happen. This is done by a combination of language design (and possible subtle redefinition of certain limited areas) and adoption of suitable techniques (see Rohl [2] fastback, slowback). In Pascal a one-symbol look ahead is sufficient to chose the correct alternative. Hence it is easy to combine recognising language constructs with generating code for them, without any risk of having to go back and restart parts of the analysis. Pascal compilers usually use a method of top down parsing known as 'recursive descent'. Further details of this method can be found in [12]. In order to generate code, which is the purpose of the compilation process, meaning must be given to the particular form of the language constructs which are recognised. Thus, in addition to determining that an expression is well formed, we must also check on the type of the symbols involved, arrange references to subscripted variables and ultimately generate code. This kind of processing which gives meaning to the language recognised is termed semantic processing, and is undertaken by semantic routines or procedures.

Thus we see when processing declarations in Pascal S that symbol names are entered into the symbol table together with type information. Further, as symbols are entered, the offset into what will be the stack frame is updated, thus giving us the address associated with the symbol. The procedure ENTER declared in BLOCK takes care of this work in Pascal S. A corresponding procedure LOC is used to locate identifiers in the table when they are encountered in executable statements.

At appropriate points we will need to generate code, the low level instructions which will be executed in order that the user may 'run' his program. Generation of code in Pascal S is undertaken by the procedures EMIT, EMIT1, EMIT2, which simply generate the low level instructions with different numbers of operands. In principle, code generation can be straightforward, but the code generated may take several forms and it is essential to be aware of this.

It is too easy to assume that a compiler which is being executed on a particular machine will generate code for that machine. This is not necessarily true, but if it were, what does it mean? A compiler may produce as its output an assembly language program which must then be processed by an assembler, a relocatable binary program which must undergo processing by a relocating loader (consolidator, linkage editor), or an absolute binary program which is located in a fixed place in memory and then directly executed. While examples exist of compilers producing these different forms, compilers producing relocatable binary code are more usual. However, observe that all three forms are machine specific. In other words, in generating one of these forms we need to know something about the hardware of the machine on which it is to run; such things as the number of accumulators, index registers, addressing ranges, special registers, are important because they must be exploited if the compiled code is to be even moderately efficient. However, code does not need to be generated for a specific hardware environment. An approach which has slowly become popular is that of causing the compiler to generate code for a hypothetical machine, and then writing a program on a particular machine which will interpret (decode and obey) the instructions for the hypothetical machine. This is the approach adopted in Pascal S, and also in Pascal P (see Berry [18]). The hypothetical machine has no accumulators in the conventional sense – it is stack oriented. This means that all data manipulation takes place on top of the stack; for example, if two items are to be added together, they are first loaded on the stack, an add instruction is issued which adds the two elements on the top of the stack, leaving the result as the top element of the stack. Use of such a stack machine considerably simplifies the code generation process since we do not need to concern ourselves about optimum use of registers and accumulators, which can be a complex matter.

One topic which has not so far received much attention is that of dealing with expressions. Historically it was this matter which focused attention on the need to provide a compiler or formula translator. An efficient method of treating expressions so that they may be rapidly evaluated at run time is important, in that it will play a significant part in determining the efficiency of the compiler as a whole. The important thing to remember about expressions is that they cannot simply be evaluated by a left to right scan, for in most cases this would ignore 'priority of operators' which is normally assumed. For example, it would normally be assumed that the expression 4 + 3 * 2 evaluated to 10 rather than the 14 which would be obtained by ignoring the priority of the multiply. Any expression, with or without parentheses, in conventional form, which is termed infix, can be converted to an alternative parenthesis free form known as reverse polish. In this reverse polish form the expression can be evaluated simply with the correct operator priority. The conversion from infix form to reverse polish or postfix form is achieved by a simple algorithm which uses a stack to hold the operators. It was in this context that the idea of a stack or symbol cellar was first discovered and exploited. The algorithm for the conversion requires that we associate a priority with each operator as follows

Operator	priority
+ –	1
*/	2

(the list of operators and priorities can of course be extended or changed as and when appropriate). Let us assume a string of input symbols 'instring', of which the current element is 'item', and an operator stack 'stack', of which the last element is 'top'.

If 'item' is an identifier or numeric constant, transcribe it directly to the output string. If 'item' is a left parenthesis, PUSH it onto 'stack'. If 'item' is an operator (one of '(',')', '+', '–', '*', '/'), compare its priority with the priority of the operator at the top of the operator stack. If the priority of 'item' exceeds

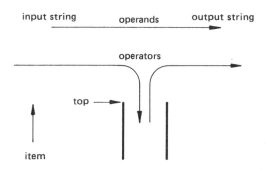

Fig. 5.1 – Converting infix to reverse polish.

the priority of 'top', then PUSH 'item' onto stack and continue, but in the event that the priority of 'top' exceeds or is equal to the priority of 'item', then POP items from the stack into the output string until an operator appears at 'top' with lesser priority than 'item'. As before, transcribe 'item' to stack and continue. When 'item' is a right parenthesis, items are copied from 'stack' to the output string until a left parenthesis is obtained. Both parentheses are then discarded. After processing the last item of the input string, the remaining items in 'stack' are popped and added to output string. A Pascal version of this algorithm is given here in program POLISH.

```
program polish;

const    maxin   =40;
         maxout  =40;
         maxstack=40;

type     stores = array[0..maxout] of char;

var      instring: string[maxin];
         outstring, stack: stores;
         operandset, operatorset: set of char;
         out, top, lastout, lastin, item: integer;
         discard: char;

procedure PUSH(it: char);
begin
   if top < maxstack
   then begin
      top:=top+1;
      stack[top]:=it
   end else begin
      writeln('stack overflow');
      exit(polish)
   end
end;   { PUSH }
```

```
function POP: char;
begin
  if top > 0
  then begin
    POP:=stack[top];
    top:=top-1
  end else begin
    writeln('stack underflow');
    exit(polish)
  end
end; { POP }

procedure MOVE(it: char);
begin
  if it = '('
  then begin
    writeln(' unmatched bracket ');
    exit(polish)
  end else if lastout<maxout
            then begin
              lastout:=lastout+1;
              outstring[lastout]:=it
            end else begin
              writeln('output string full');
              exit(polish)
            end
end; { MOVE }

function PRIORITY(it: char): integer;
begin
  case it of
  ')','%' : PRIORITY:=-1;
      '(' : PRIORITY:= 0;
  '+','-' : PRIORITY:= 1;
  '*','/' : PRIORITY:= 2;
      '^' : PRIORITY:= 3;
  end {case}
end; { PRIORITY }

procedure PUSHorMOVE(its: char);

var    itemtostack: boolean;
begin
  if its = '('
  then PUSH(its)
  else if its = ')'
          then begin
            while PRIORITY(stack[top]) <> PRIORITY('(') do MOVE(POP);
            discard:=POP
          end else if its in operatorset
                  then repeat
                    itemtostack:=PRIORITY(its) > PRIORITY(stack[top]);
                    if itemtostack
                    then PUSH(its)
                    else MOVE(POP)
                  until itemtostack
                  else begin
                    writeln(' invalid operator ',its);
                    exit(polish)
                  end
end; {PUSHorMOVE}

begin {main}
  lastin:=0;
  operatorset:=['%','+','-','*','/','^'];
  operandset :=['a'..'z','0'..'9'];

  while lastin<>1 do
  begin

    gotoxy(8,4);write(' type an expression .. ');
```

```
readln(instring); lastin:=length(instring);
gotoxy(31,5);
item:=0;        lastout:=-1;
stack[0]:='%';    top:=0;

repeat
  item:=item+1;
  if instring[item] in operandset
  then MOVE(instring[item])
  else if instring[item] in (operatorset + ['(',')'])
       then PUSHorMOVE(instring[item])
       else begin
         writeln('illegal symbol ',instring[item]);
         gotoxy(31,6);
         item:=lastin
       end
until item=lastin;

while top>0 do MOVE(POP);           { purge stack }

for out:=0 to lastout do write(outstring[out]);
end { while }


end.
```

When the input string is (b*b − 4*a*c)/(2*a)

the output string is bb*4a*c*−2a*/

Such postfix expressions are evaluated by scanning from the left for the first operator; immediately to its left are the two operands so that an evaluation of part of the expression can take place. The result is a new operand. The next operator to the right is located and applied to the operands on its left. This is repeated until evaluation is complete. It should be observed that an expression in postfix form is ideally suited for evaluation by a stack oriented machine as described earlier. For, if the presence of an operand is taken to be a directive to load it onto the stack, and if the presence of an operator is taken to mean perform this operation on the top of the stack, then it should be clear that the result of the evaluation will be left at the top of the stack. Not surprisingly Pascal S, which has the type of run time stack envisaged here, rearranges expressions into reverse polish form for evaluation, but the manner in which this is done may not be obvious to the reader. This is because the analysis of and generation of code for an expression is undertaken principally by the procedures EXPRESSION, SIMPLEXPRESSION, TERM, and FACTOR, which are closely related and indirectly recursive. Because they are recursive, intermediate results are held *behind the scenes* on the run time stack of whatever is executing the compiler, and hence no explicit manifestation of the stack which was used in the reverse polish algorithm is apparent in the compiler.

In considering Pascal S we are exploring a relatively simple compiler. Its assumption of a stack oriented run time environment, which leads to simple code generation and straightforward expression evaluation, cannot be made by all compilers. Nonetheless in examining the principles of operation of such a complex artefact as a compiler, it helps to omit topics that are not directly needed in the compiler under examination. That is not to say that these topics can be ignored, but rather that they can be considered when some of the more fundamental issues have been examined and are understood.

EXERCISES

1. Which of the procedures EXPRESSION, SIMPLEEXPRESSION, TERM, FACTOR, are used in processing the statement.

    $$r:=(b*b - 4*a*c)/2*a) ?$$

    In what order are the procedures called, and what code does each generate?

2. For each of the expressions given below decide whether it is syntactically correct and/or semantically correct in Pascal S. Give reasons for your answers.

    $$-(a>b) \underline{\text{or}} \ (c<d)$$
    $$(a=b) \ + \ (c=d)$$
    $$a>b \underline{\text{and}} \ a<c$$
    $$'A' \ * \ 'B'$$

    (assume a, b, c, d, are all defined as integers).

3. Explain the role played by the 'normal' field of TAB in the body of procedure FACTOR.

4. Identify at least five of the Pascal S error codes which flag semantic rather than syntactic errors.

5. The ability to use expressions after the symbol '=', in the definitions which follow const in a Pascal program, would be a convenience for the user, but a nuisance to the compiler writer. Explain why.

Chapter 6

Run Time Support

6.1 EXECUTION OR INTERPRETATION?

The result of the compilation process will be an *object program*. Previous consideration has been given to the forms that this object code may take. In brief these forms may result in the direct execution of the object code on a specific machine (i.e. the instructions generated have been part of the low level instruction set of that machine), or it may result in the interpretation of the object code by a suitable program residing in the host machine. The Pascal S system which has been used as an example throughout is an interpretive system. A program compiled by the Pascal S compiler must be executed by the Pascal S interpreter as embodied in the procedure INTERPRET. The only drawback to this approach is that the execution time required by interpretive systems is usually longer than that required by directly executed systems. Perhaps more important than considerations of execution speed or space required at run time, are considerations of run time support. These can embrace such topics as the library of procedures or functions available to the user program, and the provision of adequate error handling and diagnostic facilities. The first topic, that of library support is one on which Pascal has attracted much criticism. This is because early Pascal implementations denied (intentionally) the possibility of a user incorporating pre-compiled procedures or functions into his program. Later implementations of Pascal compilers have attempted, in various ways, to permit this. Of more direct concern to the compiler writer, since it is his responsibility, is the provision of run time diagnostics. User's experiences here will differ widely, but what is provided in this area ranges from the pathetic to the pleasing. The least satisfactory form of run time diagnostic support is the one which simply reports to the high level language user 'error at location ?????', where the location given represents perhaps the entry or exit point of a subroutine used by the compiler writer. Such reports are frustrating to the high level language user, since considerable time and effort is often needed to identify such errors. A high level language user has the right to expect his own errors to be reported back in terms of the program he wrote and the symbols he used.

This may not be easy, and it may be inefficient in either execution speed or in space utilisation, but it is the goal which should be aimed for. At compile time a listing of the source program should be produced, and this should have line numbers for each source line added to it, so that both run time and compile time errors can be referred back to the source line which caused the error. It is also desirable to be able to report back for any arithmetic errors, say, which user symbols had erroneous or out of range values. However, the names of all symbols must be carried through to the run time environment in order that this may happen. This is not often done since this means passing the symbol table across from compile time to run time and this can be a significant overhead. Note, however, that this is done in the Pascal S system and thus one is able to provide sensible and adequate run time diagnostics which refer to user symbols. The trace is another facility which can be extremely helpful to the user. An indication of, say, the last hundred statements executed together with the values of all accessible variables at time of failure can be extremely helpful. In order to provide this, a constantly refreshed list of the statements which have been executed must be maintained, and this will inevitably slow down execution speed. This is therefore commonly made the subject of a switch or directive so that the user may or may not use it, as he wishes. The essential point is that the diagnostic facilities should be built in so that they may be used rather than omitted, so that the user has no option.

Little was said about diagnostics at compile time and that omission can be rectified here. At various points in the work previously described, there was the possibility of providing excellent error diagnostics. The empty entries in the finite state table could have pointed to quite specific error messages indicating the error which had occurred; in the bottom up analysis the occurrence of a symbol which could not lead to the goal or sub goal required, and so on. The opportunity for providing meaningful error indicators is there. The compiler writer should offer the user as much as he can. An interesting account of what can (should) be done, and the different philosophies which may be adopted in error reporting and recovery is given by Horning [3] in "What the compiler should tell the user".

The run time support provided for the Pascal S user is fairly easily seen by examining the procedure INTERPRET. Much of the work of this procedure is straightforward, and much has already been described in considering the operation of the run time stack. Hence an overview of what the run time processing entails can be quickly obtained, though some of the detail may be more difficult to comprehend. The number of different instructions which the compiler can generate is small, nevertheless a limited though very useful high level language has been built upon these instructions. On machines with large instruction sets it is often difficult for compiler writers to exploit the wide variety of instructions available.

Finally it remains to observe that a compiler is simply a program - one which requires high level language programs as input and produces a version of the source in a lower level language as output. It is useful to consider a compiler from two points of view, that of user and that of compiler writer, so that requirements of one and the restrictions on the other may, to some extent, be recognised. Easy access to a compiler written in a high level language helps considerably, since algorithms and techniques can be seen as part of a compiling system and not simply examined in isolation. As a result, both the text, and the examples, make many references to Pascal S. The author's view is that the limitations inherent in examining one compiling system in detail are compensated by the easier understanding of the particular rather than the general.

EXERCISES

1. Briefly describe what changes are necessary to the compiler, and to the interpreter of Pascal S, in order that additional standard procedures or functions may be provided.

2. Describe the information printed by the *post mortem dump* facility of the Pascal S interpreter. What further information could usefully, and easily, be provided?

3. Why is there little opportunity for the Pascal S interpreter to provide input/output diagnostic information?

4. A retroactive trace will print, after a run time failure, a limited number of the most recently executed instructions. Comment on whether, and how, such a trace facility could be implemented in the Pascal S interpreter.

5. Some run time support packages will print, for each source statement of the user's program, the number of times it was executed prior to failure. (See Watt and Findlay in [9]). Discuss whether one or more of the unused operation codes might be used to provide 'statement markers', in order that such a facility be available for Pascal S.

Chapter 7
Assemblers

Programming a computer at a 'low level' could perhaps mean producing a bit pattern representing an instruction in each word of as many words of memory as is necessary to construct a program. However, this would be very tedious. One would not contemplate writing the instructions in binary, but possibly in octal or hexadecimal. It is still a tiresome task to contemplate. The resulting program would doubtless contain many errors. Two factors contribute to make this type of programming very uneconomic. The first is that it is rather easier for people to remember instructions as names, such as <u>load</u> or <u>add</u>, than it is to remember the octal or decimal equivalents. The second and more important factor is to know the address to which any jump is made. To achieve this, we must consider our instructions to be stored in specific memory locations so that all necessary addresses can be computed. If we proceed in this way, however, the difficulties which can arise in modifying a program become considerable. In particular, insertion of an instruction requires that subsequent instructions must change their location, with the attendant risk that many jump instructions now jump to the wrong instruction. It is possible to write programs in this way, but it should be obvious why people who programmed like this (because there was no alternative) spent some time looking for 'a better way'. Using an assembly language and its assembler *is* a better way.

An assembly language program consists of instructions, which are considered machine executable, and directives, which enable the user to control the action of the assembler. An assembler takes such a program as its input and produces as output a listing of the source instructions indicating the octal or hexadecimal equivalents, together with a version of the program which can be loaded into memory and executed. Thus we may say an assembler converts a source program into a listing and a binary program. This of course is simplification, but it will serve as the basis for further remarks.

A simple assembler will assume that a user's instructions are to be stored from a particular memory location onwards. The user can change this default value by using a suitable directive within the program. But since a specific or absolute address in memory is being used by default or by directive, the resulting output from the assembler is a program in absolute binary code. A program in this form can be a big nuisance, because the user, who is not necessarily the program writer, needs to know which memory locations are used, so that the program does not corrupt and is not corrupted by anything else in memory. A second reason why the production of absolute binary code is not a good idea is associated with programming style. It was recognised many years ago that rather than writing and assembling one large program it was easier and more sensible to write and use a collection of smaller program segments, where such segments may or may not be subroutines. This philosophy has the added advantage that segments may be used in several programs and made available to other users. In this situation it is a distinct disadvantage to have segments which must be located in a particular area of memory. It is much more useful to write an assembly language program which does not make assumptions about where it is in memory and to cause the assembler to produce code which may be loaded and executed in any part of memory. Such code is called relocatable binary code.

The preceding overview of the assembly process has served to introduce some terms and concepts. A closer examination of the work done by an assembler can now be undertaken.

In examining the work of a compiler we started by considering the alphabet that could be used in constructing the source program. This can also usefully be done for an assembler.

The upper case letters and the digits will always be the principal elements of the alphabet, but use will be made of special characters in many assemblers. Having decided what characters may appear as input, we need to consider what form the source program might take. We may perhaps consider a typical instruction to consist of the following fields.

⟨label field⟩   ⟨operator field⟩   ⟨operand field⟩

where the operand field may contain several operands. Because punched cards have been popular as a means of input, an assembler will often expect input to be in fixed format. That is, as well as being able to assume one instruction per card, we may also assume that the three fields mentioned above will occur in specific columns of the card. These assumptions are inconvenient when the principal source of input is intended to be an on-line terminal. In this case it is clearly better to take one or more particular characters as delimiting each of the three fields. While under this sytem it would be easy to envisage writing more than one instruction per line, this is rarely done by users and is often deemed to be unacceptable to the assembler. Input in this form is termed free format, although experience shows that many users adopt a 'fixed' format approach even when this is not necessary, because this considerably enhances the readability of a program. A feature usually available to a user is the ability to append a comment to each source line following the operand field. This can also improve considerably the intelligibility of the program to other users, although such comments are of course ignored by the assembler.

Having due regard to the different characters which may legally appear in the input, and to the format of the input, the assembler must recognise each of the three possible fields of instruction if they are present. Each field may be thought of as consisting of tokens. If there is a label, then it will be in the appropriate columns of a card or it will be followed by a delimiter (the colon character ':' is often used) which determines that the preceding symbol was a label. Whether or not a label exists, the next field to be recognised is that of the operator or instruction mnemonic. Like the label field, this field will simply consist of a name, and, in the case of the instruction name, this will usually be a three, four or five character name. A space character will usually delimit the instruction mnemonic, then will follow either immediately or in the appropriate columns, the operand field. Since it may consist of one or more references to accumulators, special registers, memory locations or other operands, this field will require much more analysis than either of the preceding fields. This analysis will be described later.

As output, our assembler will usually be required to produce a listing of the source program processed, which gives both the source statements and their assembled equivalents in addition to a machine code version of the program. This code is the bit pattern which, when loaded into memory, represents the original source program. In whatever form this machine code is stored (paper tape, cards, or magnetic media) it can easily be corrupted. To guard against this, the assembler generates the code as a series of blocks of modest size, each of which includes 'housekeeping' information such as the number of words in the block and a checksum. Such information is needed in order to preserve the integrity of the binary program. Few generalisations can usefully be made about the format of the binary code produced by an assembler.

The task to be performed by the assembler has been outlined. What must now be considered in more detail is *how* this task is to be performed. First consider the processing associated with each field as it is encountered in a left to right scan of each line of source input.

7.1 THE LABEL FIELD

The label, if any, which precedes an instruction is a user-defined symbol. As such it must follow the rules prescribed for such symbols in the assembler concerned. How many characters are significant? What characters are legal in a user symbol? Provided all appropriate rules are satisfied, the appearance of a label constitutes the definition of the symbol, and accordingly both the symbol and the associated value must be entered in the symbol table. But what do we mean by the value associated with a symbol? Consider the following in Figure 7.1.

.

.

.

.

DOUBLE: ADD   1,2   ; add accumulator 1 to acc 2

          JUMP   EXIT

LIMIT = 6

EXIT: SUBTRACT 1,1   ; subtract acc 1 from acc 1

.

.

.

.

.

Figure 7.1

There are three user symbols in the example and of these LIMIT is used in a different way to DOUBLE, and EXIT. These last two specifically label instructions and their value will be the memory address at which these instructions reside. In contrast LIMIT is defined as a constant rather than an instruction and its value is the constant, rather than the address in memory where the constant is stored. Hence when a label is encountered we can enter the label in the symbol table. However, an examination of the instruction field is necessary before the value of the label can be entered in the table.

It is easy to assume that the definition of a label will precede its use, but this is frequently not the case, as the example given earlier illustrates. A reference to EXIT appears before its definition. This is termed a forward reference or a branch ahead. In order that the assembled version of the instruction JUMP EXIT may be produced we need to have processed the definition of EXIT. We can do this if the assembler makes two passes through the source text. The first pass will be used only to identify all label definitions and make a suitable entry into the symbol table for each. On the second pass the instruction processing proper can be undertaken. If in this second pass a reference to an undefined label is encountered, then special action may be necessary. Solving the forward reference problem in this way has led us to a two-pass assembler — the classical assembler. However we should observe that this is not the only way to deal with the forward reference problem. Instead we could make use of a branch ahead table to store information about those labels which were used in advance of their definition. This will enable us to use a one-pass assembler if the branch ahead table is included in the binary output from the assembler. Thus we force the loader to do the work which is in other circumstances done by the assembler.

In using the branch ahead table, note is kept of the next free element. When a forward reference is encountered the symbol is entered into the symbol table. Since the symbol has "no value", the current free element position of the branch ahead table is entered into the symbol table, together with a flag which will distinguish this entry from a genuine value. The memory reference to the instruction using the forward reference is kept, together with a chain pointer in the branch ahead table. For the first forward reference to this symbol the chain pointer will be set to some easily distinguishable value. For subsequent entries the "value" entry for the symbol from the symbol table will be copied into the branch ahead table, before the value entry in the symbol table is updated, as was indicated earlier. When the definition of the symbol is found, the chain could be used to insert the correct value of the symbol in all instructions which referred to it. But this assumes we have easy access to all such instructions. More realistically we should assume that we have been writing a version of the binary program to filestore as it is created. If this is so then it will not, in general, be possible to unchain the entries which follow the definition of a symbol. Thus the value of the symbol and the last reference to it will be preserved and passed to a loader which will resolve all forward references using the branch ahead table.

Inventing meaningful labels in an assembly program can be just as tedious for the programmer as it is time consuming for the assembler to deal with them. Because many labels may be needed, many of which are too insignificant to be worthy of a special name, it is better that the assembly language provide facilities which recognise this. The reader is referred to the discussion of local labels. in Knuth [15].

7.2 SYMBOL TABLE ORGANISATION

We observed earlier that one of the advantages to the user of using an assembly language was the facility to define and use symbolic names. This implies that the assembler creates and uses a symbol table. As we noticed when studying the compilation process, there are a variety of ways of gaining access to a symbol table depending upon the assumptions, if any, one may make about the ordering of the symbols or their distribution through the alphabet. Rather than repeat these discussions, the user is referred back to the appropriate section. For the user–defined symbols of an assembler, a hashed entry table can be used. The requirement that this table needs to be larger than the number of symbols expected is less embarrassing here than in other circumstances, because the amount of information associated with any symbol to be stored is modest, being the symbol itself, its value and an indication of the way it is to be used. In a two-pass assembler such a table organisation would be sufficient, whilst for a one-pass assembler the symbol table would need to be augmented by the branch ahead table, for reasons given earlier.

7.3 THE OPERATOR OR INSTRUCTION FIELD

Whether or not we encounter a label field, we can expect to locate an operator field, that is, an instruction mnemonic. This must be recognised as a legal mnemonic, and a binary version of an instruction of this form must ultimately be constructed. There must be an instruction mnemonic for each of the machine instructions to which a user has access. In consequence the set of usable mnemonics can be easily identified. There are several ways of recognising instruction mnemonics. They may, like user-defined symbols, be stored in a hashed entry table. If this is done then these entries must be inserted as part of the table initialisation, since they are used but not defined. This approach has much to commend it, since all symbols are kept in one table, and any attempt by the user to use one of the instruction mnemonics as his own symbol should lead to error. However, since the instruction mnemonics are all known in advance they could be sorted and set up in a table of their own. Access could then be by the binary chop method outlined in the discussion of symbol tables for compilers. Equally if the instruction mnemonics are such that their first characters are evenly distributed through the alphabet, this information could be used for some other form of rapid access. A consideration of the instruction mnemonics of one or two assemblers will however reveal that this latter suggestion is not often helpful. Whichever approach is adopted, all that is required is that an instruction mnemonic be rapidly located in order that it may be replaced by its equivalent in suitable binary form.

Not all items in the instruction field undergo the same treatment. When we say that an instruction mnemonic is replaced by its binary equivalent, we are assuming that what has been recognised is an instruction with a machine level equivalent. However, in order to provide additional help to the user, assemblers frequently offer facilities in the form of pseudo-operations (pseudo-ops); that is a mnemonic which appears in the instruction field but which has no binary counterpart. Also in this category are assembly directives which the user may use to control the way the assembler operates. Perhaps because their format is similar, a distinction between pseudo operations and assembly directives is not always made but, for illustrative purposes, we observe that in the Plan assembler for 1900 machines a pseudo operation appears to be a single operation when it is in fact replaced by several instructions. Others call this a macro instruction. In contrast an assembly directive can easily be recognised. Thus END is likely to be the directive which causes assembly to cease, while for example, RADIX 8, could be a directive to consider every numeric constant from this point to be written in octal. The reader could perhaps supply other examples from the assembly language with which he is most familiar. Directives will usually be preceded by a special character '·', or '#' for example, which makes them easily recognisable to both the reader and the assembler. The repertoire of directives varies considerably from assembler to assembler, but one class of directives deserves a special mention, namely those which allow the user to modify what may be known as the permanent symbol table, or the symbol table which holds the instruction mnemonics. The user will often be allowed to delete entries from and add entries to the table. This is a useful facility. For example a floating point processor may be an optional extra on a minicomputer. If it is not installed then it is pointless allowing the assembler to generate floating point instructions. This is easily done by not including the relevant mnemonics in the assembler's symbol table. If subsequently the floating point processor is installed, the appropriate entries can be added to the symbol table. If facilities to add mnemonics to or remove them from a symbol table are available in an assembler, then they are easier to implement in one using a hashed entry table than in one which uses a table of ordered entries. This is because the table usually has to be reordered.

Having recognised the mnemonic in the instruction field and taken suitable action it now remains to consider the third and most awkward field, the operand field.

7.4 THE OPERAND FIELD

This field causes a few more problems in processing because it generally has several sub-fields. The number of sub-fields will be related to instruction type and ultimately to the architecture of the machine. Thus whilst it is useful to identify possible operand fields from the instruction categories, such as register, register to store, register to indexed store and so on, such classifications assume a two-address processor. In reality our assembler may be for a one-address machine or a three-address machine and thus the details of the processing required for what has been termed the operand field may vary considerably. Recognising this we observe that the details may change but the principles do not; so let us assume where appropriate that we are dealing with a two-address machine.

After the instruction mnemonic has been recognised, the form of instruction skeleton required for the instruction being processed will be known. Hence we also know what form our operand field will take. Consider the instructions in Figure 7.2.

LOAD   2, SEVEN

ADD   2, 1

STORE   1,RESULT+2

JUMP   *—6

Figure 7.2

These provide a simple illustration of the kind of operand fields which may be encountered. The load and store instructions refer to an accumulator and a storage location. The add refers to two accumulators while the jump instruction uses the current location counter ,*, to refer to an address.

References to accumulators are usually explicit; hence the digit must be recognised and a check made that it is a valid reference. In the example given a comma delimits one operand sub-field from another. If this delimiting is not done by a particular character then it must be done, as we observed earlier, by using different column positions on a card. The item of greatest difficulty in processing the operand field is an expression. Remember that in dealing with expressions in a high level language, our processing was intended to verify that the expression was well formed, and to rearrange it so that it could be correctly evaluated when the user program was executing. In the assembly process when an expression is encountered it must, if it is well formed, be evaluated by the assembler. Because of this the forms of expression allowed by an assembly language will often be severely restricted. An expression can most easily be processed by a left to right scan but this will mean that priority normally associated with operators is lost. As a result 2+3*5 will produce 25 rather than 17. As long as this is made clear it is tolerable, although not ideal. If normal priority of operands is to be maintained then the assembler must use a stack to process the expression. This is not usually done. An expression consisting simply of explicit numerical constants causes no problems. However, when user-defined symbols appear in expressions more care is required. If the symbol has already been defined then its value can be retrieved from the symbol table and used in the expression if appropriate. But what if the user name has not yet been defined? Some assemblers will say that this possibility must not arise (e.g. MIX [15], Plan [16]) so that they may complete their work in one pass. Naturally in a two pass assembler the situation will not occur.

Thus for the simple situations envisaged so far it can be seen that recognition of a particular instruction mnemonic will make clear what kind of operand field is expected. The sub-fields of the operand field can be identified and their values stored in appropriate fields of the binary instruction being created.

Nothing has yet been said about whether the assembler is to produce absolute or relocatable binary output. Attention must now be given to this topic. If we assume that an absolute binary program is being produced then either the user has indicated by means of an assembly directive where the program will reside in memory, or the default setting has been assumed. In either case one can assign to those labels which label instructions an absolute memory address. Whether such a label is used alone or in an expression in the operand field, it will be possible to check that the result is always a legal address, since such an expression can be completely evaluated at assembly time. Thus producing absolute binary code is straightforward but, as was outlined earlier, it is less useful than producing relocatable binary code, where the assembler cannot complete all necessary processing. The strategy invariably employed here is for the assembler to collect information in the form of tables and for these to be passed in the relocatable binary output to the loader where all processing will be completed.

In producing relocatable binary code the assembler rarely deals with particular memory addresses. Thus in contrast to the earlier situation in which one could associate a memory address with a label which labelled an instruction, the assembler only ever associates a relative address with such a label when producing relocatable code. In other words the label is regarded as being relative to, say, the first instruction of the program. The value of a label can thus be regarded as consisting of two parts, an absolute part and a relocatable part whose value is unknown at assembly time. Normally this relocatable part will simply be the address of the first instruction of the program, but its precise value will be determined by the loader. Clearly this will make a difference to our assembler work because it will not now be possible to evaluate completely expressions which involve relocatable items. This can only be done when the value of the relativizer (the relocatable part) is determined. Thus in order that our assembler can satisfactorily produce a relocatable binary, certain modifications must be made to the outline processing strategy presented earlier. These modifications are entirely concerned with our handling of user defined symbols. In the symbol table, as well as the value of the symbol, we must keep information indicating whether the value is absolute or relocatable, and if relocatable we will need to know with respect to which relativizer it is relocatable. In minicomputers for example, a limited amount of memory is directly addressable from any part of a program. Typically this might be the first 256 words of memory. Constants and other items to which frequent reference is made will be stored here and the user symbols referring to these items will be 'page zero relative' since this first 256 words is often termed page zero. User symbols referring to items stored in an area of memory other than page zero are relocatable with respect to some other relativizer. If this information is simply stored in the symbol table then the implication is that it is used where the symbols are used, i.e. in expressions. Consider the program skeleton in Figure 7.3.

When treating this as an absolute assembly the expressions RESULT+2, *–6 could be completely evaluated. Let us designate the first instruction of the program as 'fip', if RESULT is 27 instructions later, then the 'value' of RESULT is fip+27. Equally if the JUMP instruction is 56 instructions after the first instruction then * (the current location pointer) is fip+56. Hence the two expressions above become fip+27+2, and fip+56–6 respectively. The result of evaluating each of these expressions is a relocatable part and an absolute part. It should be clear that the result of evaluating an expression which only uses the operators plus or minus is only acceptable if it is either absolute or consists of one relativizer (fip in the above examples) and an absolute part. Any other outcome is designated 'malformed'. In expressions where multiply and divide

```
                ; We assume that each instruction when
                ; assembled occupies one memory location.
                ; loc)        label      operation

    fip  +   0)   START:      SUBTRACT  0,0     ; clear accumulator
    fip  +   1)               SUBTRACT  1,1
                                 .
                                 .

                                 .
    fip  +  24)               ADD       0,1     ; add accumulators
    fip  +  25)               STORE     1,RESULT+2
    fip  +  26)               RETURN            ; subroutine exit
    fip  +  27)   RESULT:     0
                                 .
                                 .

                                 .
    fip  +  56)               JUMP         *-6
                              Figure 7.3
```

are permitted, the appearance of a symbol designated as 'relative' or 'relocatable' as an operand of multiply or divide will immediately render the expression malformed.

The assembler must ensure that wherever a user defined symbol which requires a relativizer is used, the absolute part is stored in the appropriate field of the instruction and that a note is kept (flag is set) that a relativizer needs to be added. Then, when the loader is loading this instruction or any others into memory, the appropriate relativizer can be added. In this way the evaluation of an expression may be completed.

So far it has been assumed, although not explicitly stated, that an entire program is being assembled at once; in other words that all symbols used were defined in the program being assembled. In the introduction it was stated that it helped to be able to assemble segments or sub programs separately and then combine the already assembled parts satisfactorily into one program. This principle makes possible the easy use of a library of already assembled segments or subroutines which can be of significant help in the rapid construction of working programs. In order that segments of programs may be satisfactorily combined in this way, a formalised method of inter segment communication must be adopted.

7.5 INTER SEGMENT COMMUNICATION

For any user-defined symbol encountered in a program we are interested in both its definition and its use. What cannot be tolerated in a two-pass assembler is a symbol about which nothing is known. But if this symbol is the name of a subroutine in one already assembled segment to which we wish to jump from the segment being assembled, how can we know anything of the symbol? The answer lies in providing assembly directives which allow the user to define a symbol as one which is a subroutine entry point which may be referred to in other segments or, to indicate that a symbol is used in this segment but defined in another segment. Thus

.ENTRY   PRINT

could be a directive indicating that the label PRINT was an entry point defined in this segment which might be used in other segments. whilst

.EXTERNAL ERROR

could be a directive indicating that the symbol ERROR will be used in this segment but will be defined in another. This mechanism, or something similar, will suffice to provide a limited but formal means of communication between segments. How does this affect the processing we have already considered?

For those symbols defined in the present segment which may be used in other segments, all that is needed is to construct a table of their names, values and relativizers and include this table in the relocatable binary output. This could be called a definition table. In this way all relevant information is passed to the loader. The fact that the symbol might be used in other segments does not affect the use of the symbol in the segment in which it is defined.

In contrast, dealing with symbols which are used in one segment but defined in another can involve us in a significant amount of extra work. Clearly the least which must be done is to construct a table of their names, the position (address) in which they are used and, possibly, the relativizer assumed in their usage. (In fact the particular assembly directive is often used to indicate the relativizer so that it may not need to be assumed). This table, which may be called the *use table* must be passed to the loader in the relocatable binary output from the assembler. However, these symbols which are defined in another segment also cause us to re-examine our treatment of expressions, because this treatment did not assume the occurrence of an externally defined symbol. Recall that an earlier example illustrated how, for expressions which only involved the operators +, −, evaluation would produce a result with an absolute part and possibly a relocatable part (which was called fip). The appearance of an externally defined symbol in such an expression could be dealt with by recording in the use table whether the symbol was to be added or subtracted, and requiring the loader to undertake the operation. But could this not lead to a violation of our earlier requirement that the result should be a relativizer plus an absolute part? If care were not taken, yes! We must check either that the partial result of the expression is absolute, or that the relativizer of the external symbol matches that of the partial expression. Further, we must check that there is no possibility, if more than one external symbol is to be added, that this leads to a malformed expression because of relativizers being accumulated. This check is achieved by considering absolute symbols or constants to have value zero, relocatable symbols to have the value one, and forming the sum of these values as the expression is processed. A value other than zero or one for this sum means that the expression is malformed. In order to do this we must know or assume the relativizer for the external symbol. This may be known from the directive used to indicate that the symbol was external. If we assume that any undefined symbol is an external symbol, then the relativizer must be assumed and recorded in the use table. The loader must then check that the assumed relativizer and the actual relativizer of the symbol correspond.

Since the expressions evaluated at assembly time usually represent addresses or integer constants, it is most unlikely that the assembly language will permit a division operator in expressions. Hence the only extension necessary to our existing treatment of ⟨expression⟩ is the inclusion of multiply as an operator. In other words, our notion of expression must be extended to include product terms. It should be obvious from our previous work that in doing this the appearance of a relocatable symbol as an operand of multiply renders the expression malformed. A product term consisting only of absolute values can be evaluated and causes no problem. The problem arises with a product term consisting of one or more external symbols; any absolute terms appearing in such a product can be evaluated, but the external symbols remain. One solution is to set up yet another table, a table of products or *product use table*. In this table, each entry could consist of the external symbols to be multiplied, the absolute multiplier, and the location at which the product is required. By requiring that each symbol in the product table also had a corresponding entry in the use table, marking it as an entry in the product table rather than to be added or subtracted elsewhere, we have collected sufficient information to allow the loader to complete the expression involving product terms. Barron [14] gives an example of an algorithm which illustrates how an expression of the form envisaged here may be processed.

EXERCISES

The following questions assume that we impose the trappings of an assembly language on the Pascal S operation codes to produce SAL, the S Assembly Language. The assembler could be written in Pascal and its output processed by the Pascal S interpreter.

1.   What output must be produced by the assembler in order that the interpreter need not be changed? Is the code produced absolute or relocatable?

2. Suggest mnemonics for the Pascal S operation codes and justify the names chosen. Discuss the reasons for and against attempting to use some of the mnemonics given in Fischer [19].

3. In the assembly language SAL, an equal sign might be used to associate a value with a data item in the following way

$$
\begin{aligned}
\text{ch} &= \text{'A'} \\
\text{pi} &= 3.14159 \\
\text{message} &= \text{'program aborts'} \\
\text{limit} &= 10
\end{aligned}
$$

Discuss what action should be taken by the assembler upon encountering each of these definitions. What action is taken on subsequent references to these symbols.

4. (a) Identify the Pascal S operation codes having operands which are references into CODE.
    (b) Identify the Pascal S operation codes which require a reference to TAB, or one of the other tables, in their implementation.

5. What changes would be necessary in order that the output from the assembler could be regarded as relocatable?

Chapter 8

Macros

In principle Macro facilities can be provided in both high level and low level languages. In practice very few high level languages offer users Macro facilities, PL/1 is perhaps the best known language which does; however most manufacturers will provide Macro facilities with their Assemblers. In consequence the discussion which follows is oriented towards Macros in a low level environment.

The preceding chapter has described what an assembler must do to convert an assembly language program into a binary form. Some assemblers will offer more facilities than mentioned here, some will offer less. The items considered should represent a significant portion of the facilities offered by an assembler with which the user is familiar, and perhaps enable him to appreciate why restrictions may be imposed by the assembly language. Many computer systems offer the user a choice of assemblers so that the user may, by considering the facilities offered by each, choose the assembler he wishes to use. This recognises that the assembler is likely to be a heavily used item of software, and to burden it with too many extravagent facilities may not be efficient or economic. Assembly language programming is tedious, and facilities which significantly help the user are worth considering. Thus to provide macro facilities in an assembler is, in some respects, costly, but can be a real help to a user. A macro assembler is therefore likely to be provided with a computer system as a separate assembler.

In many assembly languages, a user will often find himself using a particular instruction sequence. This sequence may only be three or four instructions but it may be a necessary preamble for access to particular facilities, in which case it may not be appropriate to write a subroutine, but rather use a macro. A macro assembler provides the user with the facility to give a name, the macro name, to a sequence of instructions. Thereafter, whenever in the assembly process this macro name appears, it is replaced by or expanded into the instruction sequence given in the definition of the macro name. Hence the macro assembler must provide us with facilities to define macros and thereafter use them.

Consider the following example

```
.MACRO     QUAD1
ADD        1, 1
ADD        1, 1
.ENDMACRO
```

In this example it is assumed that .MACRO must be used to indicate the start of a macro definition, whilst .ENDMACRO signifies the end of the macro definition. The macro name is QUAD1 and its purpose is to replace the contents of accumulator one by four times its original content. After this definition, wherever the name QUAD1 appears in the instruction field it will be replaced by the two add instructions which comprise the macro body. Clearly this tells the assembler writer that a table of macro names and definitions must be created. This table will differ from most of the tables seen so far in that entries (macro bodies) will be of different sizes, and may be quite lengthy. If this table is kept in filestore rather than in memory, as it may be on small machines, the whole assembly process slows down. When the macro name is encountered in subsequent processing, what happens is that the assembler is directed to take its input not from the user's source program but from the macro definition table until the end of the macro definition is reached. When this happens, the input is once more from the user's source program. Even such limited macro facilities can be extremely helpful to a programmer. However, more flexibility makes them even more usable, and especially useful is the capability to pass parameters to a macro. In the preceding example it would be more sensible to provide the particular accumulator we wished to manipulate as a parameter to the macro. Macro assemblers provide parameterization facilities in different ways. Some will require that dummy parameters are given at macro definition time as used in the following definition:

```
.MACRO     QUAD       ACC
ADD        ACC,ACC
ADD        ACC,ACC
.ENDMACRO
```

Others will simply require that reference is made in the macro body to a parameter by using a special character, immediately followed by the positional number of the parameter. This would result in our example becoming

```
.MACRO     QUAD
ADD        ↑1, ↑1
ADD        ↑1, ↑1
.ENDMACRO
```

where ↑1 refers to the first parameter, and ↑2, if it were used, would refer to the second parameter. In either case, the macro call would appear in the user's program as

QUAD 1

Providing parameterization facilities means that, when the macro body is being copied from the definition table into the user's program, each parameter occurrence must be recognised and replaced by the actual parameter. This is easier to accomplish if the parameters are preceded by a special character, particularly if this character is not used anywhere else. In the second example given, this is done explicitly by the user using the '↑' symbol. In the first example it would be prudent to precede all parameter references by such a character when the macro is being stored, otherwise the search for parameters would have to be undertaken each time the macro is called, and this could be time consuming.

Without carefully considering the consequences, a user may include a labelled instruction in the macro body. Since we have said that the macro may consist of a sequence of instructions, a label may well be needed. The macro expansion strategy, as outlined so far will, if followed, result in the same label appearing in the source program wherever the macro is called. This will lead to a *duplicate label* error message being produced by the assembler. Whenever the macro is called, the macro assembler must undertake to modify all labels and references to them occuring in a macro body. A straightforward way of doing this is to keep a count of the number of times the macro definition has been used. This count could then be attached to all labels and their references upon each expansion of the macro, thus ensuring uniqueness.

Having constructed a macro to reduce the task of repeating particular instruction sequences, some macros may be constructed which themselves call other macros. We can deal with this although some assemblers will impose constraints about the depth to which macros may be 'nested' in this manner. In order to implement this facility, much greater care is needed in expanding macros. Previously we assumed that we were either in macro expansion mode or normal mode, and that leaving one state took us into the other. If macros are nested however, to leave one macro expansion may cause us to return to another. This can be easily and systematically dealt with if we increase a level number by one each time a macro expansion is required. If this expansion leads to another then the arguments of the current expansion are stored on a stack while the new expansion is undertaken. When this inner expansion is complete, the level number is reduced and the previous arguments are retrieved from the stack. Care must be taken when dealing with the actual arguments of expansion, because the arguments of an 'inner' macro may in fact be arguments of the 'outer' macro. In this case the actual arguments are obtained from the stack rather than from the program text.

If nested macros are allowed we will need to ask ourselves whether or not a macro may call itself, the answer is yes, provided we can also offer the facility of conditional assembly. In other words, if the assembler has a directive which allows a sequence of instructions to be assembled, according to some condition which can be evaluated at assembly time. Only with this facility could an endless recursion be avoided. Consider a Macro SHIFT to shift the contents of an accumulator a given number of places to the left (we assume that such an instruction is not part of the order code of the host machine):

```
;argument one gives the accumulator
;argument two gives the number of
; places to shift

.MACRO SHIFT
LSHIFT        ↑1, ↑1        ;shift accumulator left
↑2 = ↑2 − 1                 ;reduce shift count
SHIFT         ↑1, ↑2        ;call SHIFT

.ENDMACRO
```

Once called, this Macro will continue to call itself and thereby generate an endless list of shift instructions. We must be able to branch round the embedded call of SHIFT:

```
.MACRO SHIFT
LSHIFT        ↑1, ↑2

.IF ↑2 > 1
↑2 = ↑2 − 1
SHIFT         ↑1, ↑2
.ENDIF

.ENDMACRO
```

In this case the embedded call SHIFT is within the conditional assembly statement. The contents of the conditional statement are only included in the expansion whenever the number of places to shift exceeds one. Provision of conditional assembly simply requires a suitable form of instruction to be defined together with appropriate delimiters to indicate which statements are subject to the condition expressed. If the condition evaluates to true, the instructions up to the delimiter will be assembled, otherwise they are ignored.

Macro assemblers, and their more general counterpart macro processors, are a valuable and useful tool for the software engineer. The reader who is not familiar with these facilities is recommended to investigate the macro assemblers on the machines he has access to, or to consider the more general discussions in Brown [17].

Chapter 9

Loaders

Whether a program has been processed by a compiler or an assembler, the resulting machine code must at some stage be loaded into memory for execution. Before considering in detail the work which must be undertaken by the sort of loader assumed in the discussion on assemblers, the form and scope of different loaders must be briefly considered.

When a computer is switched on, an automatic program load may or may not be brought into operation. If it is not, then action needs to be taken by the user, such as pressing a button or flicking a switch; in either case the effect is to cause a fairly primitive program to be loaded from read only memory (ROM). In a more primitive environment, the user may be required to enter instructions in binary form directly into a particular area of memory, by means of appropriate switches. Since the possibility of error here is high, the number of instructions to be entered is kept to a minimum. The program entered thus may then permit paper tape or cards containing a more ambitious program to be entered. For example, input consisting of a sequence of number pairs comprising an address followed by an instruction to be stored at that address could be loaded after keying in the initial instructions. Because it contains an address for each instruction, input in this form is inconveniently bulky, and is therefore only likely to be used to load the more sophisticated *binary loader*. Let us use this term to denote a loader which would load the form of absolute binary code produced by an assembler. Such an absolute binary code might consist of a series of blocks, each one containing an indication of its type, the address at which to start loading the contents, and a checksum for the whole block. Such a loader need only distinguish between a normal block containing instructions and data, and a block which contained the address to which control would be transferred at the termination of loading, that is, the start address of the program being loaded.

We have seen that absolute binary code is of limited use on machines capable of supporting an operating system. What is needed as a minimum is a loader which can load a program into an area of memory which is dictated by the operating system rather than the program being loaded. We shall term such a

loader a *relocatable loader*. Relocatable binary code will contain address references which depend upon a particular relavitizer. It will be part of the loader's
function to identify all such occurrences, supply the value of the appropriate
relativizer, and compute the actual reference before loading the completed
instruction.

The provision of inter-segment communication facilities caused additional
work for the assembler and will also cause additional work for a loader. However, because this is such a useful facility, this work is worth undertaking. Recall
that the assembler constructed a definition table for all those symbols defined
in the segment under assembly and which were available for use by other segments. A use table of symbols used in the same segment was also constructed
but defined in another segment. For each symbol in the use table, a list of all
locations where it was used must be available. These tables are easily included
in the relocatable binary output of the assembler by designating them as
different block types to either the normal data or the start address blocks
suggested earlier. Our loader must now deal with as many segments as the user
designates, and successfully resolve all references to symbols between segments.
We note in passing that, since all programs to be executed on the machine must
pass through this load phase, and that the process may be time consuming if
there are many references to resolve, the option of preserving the output of the
loader is normally offered. Hence the loader may no longer physically load the
user's program into memory, but simply create a file in filestore which can
subsequently be easily loaded. In some environments, therefore, a *linkage
editor* or *consolidator* is the term used for what we have previously termed a
loader. In other environments the term 'relocatable loader' is used for a program which does not load a program into memory.

In addition to any segments the user may provide, usually only the *system
library* need be included in the segments to be linked. This will not normally
mean that the whole library is appended to the user program, but rather that
those segments from the library to which reference has been made by the user
will be extracted and included with his program. The resolution of references
to symbols used in segments other than those in which they are defined, is
undertaken with the help of a symbol linkage table. The definition table is
part of the relocatable binary output produced by an assembler, and when it is
recognised by the loader, all symbols from the definition table are entered into
the symbol linkage table. A hashed entry into the table is the simplest mechanism. If the symbol is not already in the table, then it should be entered, together
with its value and relativizer, if any. If the symbol is already entered in the
table, this would be because it has already been defined (in which case an error
is flagged) or because this symbol appeared in the use table of a preceding
segment. In this case all references to the symbol which have been noted in the
symbol linkage table must be identified, and if the mode is correct (i.e. the
relativizers agree) the value of the symbol is inserted where appropriate. Since

many segments may refer to a symbol before it is defined, it will be convenient to consider the symbol linkage table in two parts, one to hold the hashed entries for symbols, and the other to hold the chain of references which may precede symbol definition. Thus when encountering the use table of a segment, each entry must be hashed into the symbol linkage table. If an entry already exists for this symbol, which may be flagged as undefined, the chain of references is simply extended. If the symbol is not in the symbol table, then an entry is created and the chain started. Where the entry in the table is flagged as defined, the value of the symbol is obtained and used in all relevant locations, provided the relativizers agree. Where the use table refers to the product use table, the definition of the symbol will cause the product to be partially or fully completed. When fully completed, of course, the result can be added or subtracted at the location given in the product use table.

With references resolved, the linkage editor or relocatable loader has completed most of its work. It remains to observe that, wherever possible, the loader must use the information with which it is provided to perform error checks and consistency checks. All programs, whether processed by high level language compilers or low level assemblers, are likely to rely on the relocatable loader to complete the processing. In this respect, it is a most important piece of system software and a high standard of integrity and efficiency is expected of it.

BIBLIOGRAPHY

COMPILERS

[1] D. Gries (1971). *Compiler Construction for Digital Computers,* Wiley.
[2] J. S. Rohl (1975). *An Introduction to Compiler Writing,* Macdonald and Janes.
[3] E. L. Bauer and J. Eickel (eds.) (1974). *Compiler Construction – an advanced course,* Springer-Verlag.
[4] D. E. Knuth (1968), *The art of Computer Programming, vol. 1,* Addison Wesley.
[5] F. R. A. Hopgood and A. G. Bell (February, 1967). The Atlas Algol Preprocessor for Non-Standard Dialects, *Computer Journal,* **Volume 9, Number 4.**
[6] K. Jensen and N. Wirth (1975). *Pascal User Manual and Report,* Springer-Verlag.
[7] L. Bolliett (1968). Compiler Writing Techniques, *Programming Languages* (ed. F. Genuys), Academic Press.
[8] R. E. Berry (1978). Experience with the Pascal P Compiler, *Software Practice and Experience,* **Volume 8, Issue 5.**
[9] D. W. Barron (Ed.) (1981). *Pascal – The language and its implementation,* J. Wiley

[10] M. Daniels and S. Pemberton (1981). *Pascal Implementation,* Ellis Horwood.

[11] A. M. Addyman *(et al.),* (1979). Software Practice and Experience, **Volume 9, Issue 5.**

[12] A. J. Davie and R. Morrison (1981). *Recursive Descent Compiling,* Ellis Horwood.

[13] A. H. J. Sale (September, 1979). A Note on Scope, One-Pass Compilers, and Pascal, *Pascal News,* **15.**

ASSEMBLERS

[14] D. W. Barron (1970). *Assemblers and Loaders,* Macdonald. **Monograph 6.**

[15] D. E. Knuth (1970). *Mix,* Addison Wesley.

[16] ICL, (1967). *Plan Reference Manual,* Technical Publication **4322,** ICL.

[17] P. J. Brown (1979). *Macro Processors and Techniques for Portable Software.* John Wiley.

[18] P. Calingaert (1979). *Assemblers, Compilers and Program Translation,* Pitman.

[19] W. P. Fischer (December, 1979). Microprocessor Assembly Language Draft Standard, IEEE Task **P694/D11,** *Computer.*

PART 2

Chapter 10

Pascal S Compiler

Pascal S is from the same stable as Pascal P and the so-called 'standard' Pascal. All three were produced at E.T.H. Zurich, and all have different design goals. Pascal S is the baby of the three but is nonetheless a useful language. This language, supported by the S compiler, is not so rich as that supported by the P compiler which, in turn, is more limited than standard Pascal. Of the three compilers only the S compiler will not compile itself, since some of the language features used in its construction are not part of the S language. In particular the user may not create or use any files other than the files INPUT, OUTPUT. There are no sets, and no pointer variables, so the facilities for more general data structures are severely reduced. Statement labels accessed by goto statements are not allowed, and neither are goto statements themselves. Hence the only labels available to the user are those necessary in case statements.

The reduced language facilities are not the only feature which distinguish Pascal S from its relations. Its run time philosophy and implementation are also different. Like Pascal P, compiled programs are executed interpretively. However, unlike Pascal P, the symbolic names of user symbols are carried over to the run time environment and used there. This provides the scope for much better, and more meaningful, run time diagnostics than are possible in Pascal P.

Because of the reduced facilities outlined above, the S compiler is smaller, and therefore more easily understood, than its better equipped relations. Since the interpreter itself is written in Pascal the whole system provides, in a high level language, a useful vehicle for studying the philosophy and detail of a realistic compiler. Appreciation of the structure of this compiler will mean, because of their similarity, that the other compilers may be more easily understood.

10.1 PASCAL S SYNTAX DIAGRAMS

PROGRAM

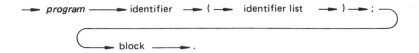

BLOCK

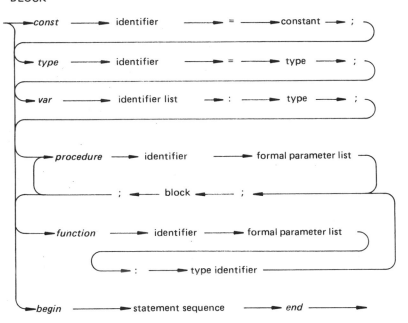

TYPE

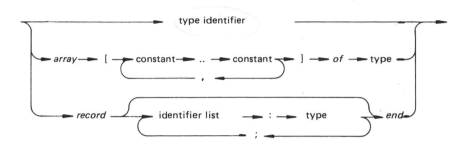

FORMAL PARAMETER LIST

IDENTIFIER LIST

IDENTIFIER

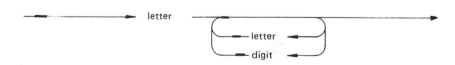

STATEMENT SEQUENCE

STATEMENT

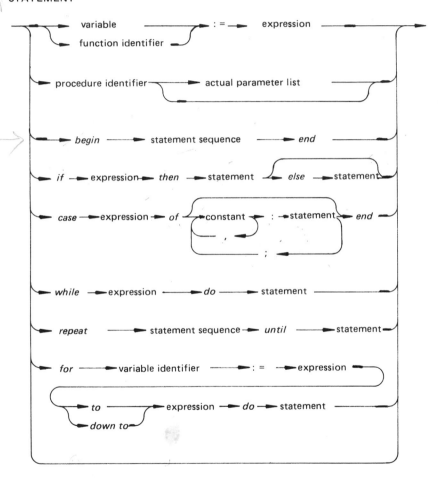

EXPRESSION

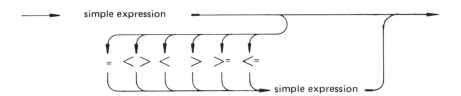

SIMPLE EXPRESSION

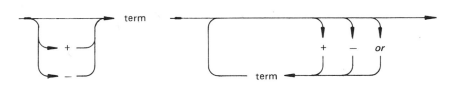

TERM

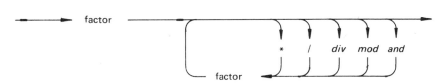

FACTOR

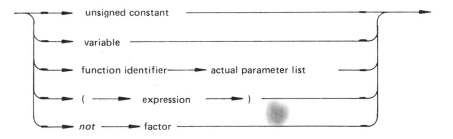

ACTUAL PARAMETER LIST

VARIABLE

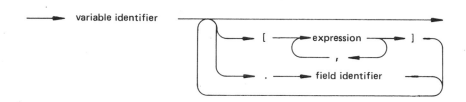

√ CONSTANT

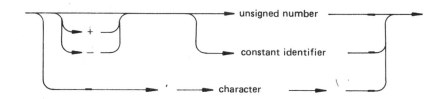

√ UNSIGNED CONSTANT

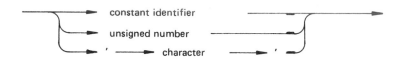

UNSIGNED NUMBER

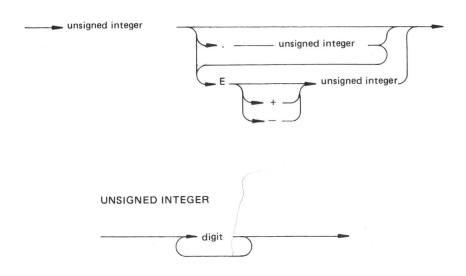

UNSIGNED INTEGER

10.2 PASCAL S COMPILER

The Pascal S compiler is modest in size but to understand its action by studying the listing is a time consuming task. To help ease this burden an overview of the principal data structures used by the compiler is given below. This is followed by a description of all the procedures of the compiler. These procedures are grouped under the titles *utilities, lexical analysis, syntax analysis, semantic routines*. However, this classification is not unique in the sense that some procedures could legitimately appear under more than one heading but they have been grouped in this way to help identify the general descriptions of the main text with specific procedures in Pascal S.

Tables used at compile time and run time.

ATAB	array table
BTAB	block table
TAB	symbol table
DISPLAY	reference to BTAB (compile time), and the stack (run time)
RCONST	holds real constants
STAB	holds string constants

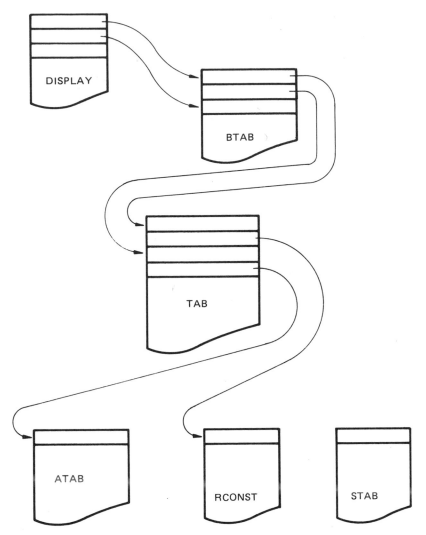

Fig. 10.1 – Diagrammatic relationship between tables at compile time.

BTAB .. index 'b'

BTAB contains one entry for every user-defined function or procedure. The first entry in the table will always have the same appearance, because it is the entry for the imaginary block surrounding every program in which all the system identifiers (standard type names, standard function names) are assumed to be defined. The second entry in the table will always be that associated with the user program. Thus, even if the user defines no procedures or functions at all, there will always be at least two entries in BTAB.

However, it is not only procedures and functions which cause entries to be made into BTAB. The identifiers used to define the fields of a record are regarded as local to that record and accordingly a record can be treated as a block. Every user defined record causes an entry in BTAB.

Each entry in BTAB consists of four items. The first is a reference to the symbol table TAB; it is designated 'last' and points to the most recent entry in TAB of an identifier declared in this block. It should be remembered that, for a procedure declaration, the name of the procedure is defined at one level, whereas its parameters and local variables are defined at the next. Two procedure names, though they may have been declared consecutively, will have their entries in the symbol table separated by such identifiers as are defined within the first of the two procedures. Hence 'last' fulfils a useful role and, as will be seen, enables all entries at one syntactic level to be chained together in the symbol table. Following 'last' in BTAB is the item 'lpar' which is also a pointer into the symbol table. 'lpar' points to the last parameter associated with the function or procedure. If there are no parameters associated with the block then 'lpar' points to the entry of the preceding function or procedure name. The last two entries in BTAB hold storage space information. 'psze' gives the number of storage units on the stack required to hold the parameters plus the housekeeping (which requires 5 units). 'vsze' gives the number of storage units required to hold the housekeeping information plus parameters plus local variables.

When the entry in BTAB concerns a record, 'lpar' and 'psze' are zero (not used), 'vsze' gives the number of storage units required to hold the record, while 'last' points to the symbol table entry for the last field of the record.

DISPLAY .. index 'level'

DISPLAY is a vector which has one entry for every block level in the user program. Since the first entry is obviously needed for the program itself, the maximum level to which procedures may be nested is one less than the number of elements in DISPLAY. The information stored in DISPLAY is a reference to BTAB. For example, when 'level' has a value of three, the third element of display points into BTAB to the name of the block currently being processed. The previous two entries in DISPLAY point to the BTAB entries of the names of the blocks which enclose the current block. When the current block has been processed, 'level' reduces by one. Thus the number of active elements in DISPLAY at any particular time reflects the level of block nesting encountered at compile time. DISPLAY adopts a different role at run time.

TAB .. index 't'

TAB is the most important table. It is created and used at compile time and is also used at run time. BTAB makes reference to TAB, while ATAB, RCONST, are referred to by TAB. Relationships are shown diagrammatically in Fig. 10.1. Every identifier defined in a user program is entered in TAB. Identifiers appear in TAB in the order of their declaration. There are eight items held for each entry in TAB:— NAME, LINK, OBJ, TYP, REF, NRM, LEV, ADR. To help limit the size of TAB, the use made of these items is not always the same, hence in certain circumstances their names may be misleading. However, a brief outline of their function is as follows:—

NAME   no more than the first ten characters of the symbol name.

LINK   a pointer to the identifier which was encountered immediately prior to this element at the same static level. For each static level the first item will have value 0 to mark the end of the chain.

OBJ   gives what might be called the 'mode' of the variable which will enable a decision to be made as to whether the symbol is being used in an appropriate context. There are five possible modes:— 0(konstant), 1(vvariable), 2(type1 user defined), 3(prozedure), 4(funktion).

NRM   NRM is boolean and is used to determine the form of load appropriate to a particular variable. For simple variables (ints, reals, bools, chars) we observe that a value parameter can be treated like a local variable. Such items will have an NRM value of 1 (true). Such items can be loaded onto the run time stack by suitable reference to their level and offset. However if a simple variable is a var parameter, all we have reference to is its address. This requires that a load address instruction be generated and this is undertaken for an NRM value of 0 (false). In a similar manner different access will be made to arrays and records according to the value of NRM. For these items we would normally wish to load their base address into the stack so that a suitable offset migh be computed. Accordingly, when an array or record is a local variable or a value parameter (NRM=1, true) we simply load its address. In the event of a variable parameter its address will reside in the parameter storage to which we have reference. Thus a straightforward load value is generated when NRM=0 (false). In short, NRM is used to determine what we load on the stack.

TYP   indicates the type of the symbol. This is indicated numerically by 0(procedure), 1(integer), 2(real), 3(boolean), 4(char), 5(array), 6(record).

REF   will usually have a value of zero but in appropriate circumstances will give a reference to other tables.

TYP=5   REF points to the relevant entry in ATAB,
TYP=6   REF points to the relevant entry in BTAB,

|OBJ=3,4   REF points to the block table entry for this procedure/function.

LEV   gives the static level at which this identifier was declared.

ADR   has a variety of uses not all of which are appropriate to the name of the item! Thus we have:—

OBJ=0   TYP=1   ADR gives actual value of constant,   *Int Const*
    0   2   ADR gives reference to value in RCONST,   *Real const*
    0   3   ADR gives ordinal # of boolean value,   *Bool. const*
    0   4   ADR gives ordinal # in character set,   *Char const.*
    2   ?   number of storage units required to hold an item of this type.

For 'field identifiers' ADR gives the offset from the start of the record in storage units, for procedures and functions it gives their start address in code, and for simple variables it gives the offset in storage units from the base of the stack frame.

For records and arrays ADR gives the number of storage units they will occupy.

For value parameters ADR gives the offset, in storage units from the stack frame base, of the first storage unit required for the item.

For var parameters it gives the offset, in storage units from the stack frame base, of the storage unit which contains the address of the actual parameter.

ATAB . . index 'a'

ATAB is the table in which information about arrays is kept. For each entry seven items of information are kept. These items are referred to as XTYP, ETYP, EREF, LOW, HIGH, ELSZ, SIZE. Strictly it should be said that these items of information are recorded for a vector. Since a multidimensional array can be considered a collection of vectors, it can be seen that there will be one entry in ATAB for each dimension of a multidimensional array. The information stored for each vector is as follows:—

XTYP   the type of the index (subscript) of the array. The only legal values that this item may have are 1(integer), 4(char).

ETYP   the type of elements of the array. This item may have values as follows:— 1(integer), 2(real), 3(boolean), 4(char), 5(array), 6(record).

EREF   in the event that ETYP has value 5(<u>array</u>), this item will refer to the element of ATAB which describes this array. In other cases it will be zero.

LOW   the value of the lower bound of the array.

HIGH   the value of the upper bound of the array.

ELSZ   the number of storage units required for each element of the array.

SIZE   the number of storage units required by the whole array.

RCONST .. index $'c2'$

This table simply holds the real constants to which the user program makes reference.

STAB .. index $'sx'$

STAB holds all the literal strings to which the user program refers.

CODE .. index $'lc'$

This array stores all the instructions which are generated by the compiler for execution at run time.

Pascal S procedure hierarchy

> Errormsg
> Endskip
> Nextch
> Error
> Fatal
> Insymbol
>> Readscale
>> Adjustscale
>> Options
>>> Switch
> Enter
> Enterarray
> Enterblock
> Enterreal
> Emit
> Emit1
> Emit2
> Block
>> Skip

Test
Testsemicolon
Enter
Loc
Entervariable
Constant
Typ
Arraytyp
Parameterlist
Constdec
Typedeclaration
Variabledeclaration
Procdeclaration
Statement
Expression (forward)
Selector
Call
Resulttype
Expression
Simpleexpression
Term
Factor
Standfct
Assignment
Compoundstatement
Ifstatement
Casestatement
Caselabel
Onecase
Repeatstatement
Whilestatement
Forstatement
Standproc
Setup
Enterids
Printtable
Interpret

10.3 PROCEDURE DESCRIPTIONS

10.3.1 Utilities

ERRORMSG Following compilation a check is made to establish whether the set 'errs' is empty. If not, ERRORMSG is called and for all elements entered into the error set by ERROR, a message is printed. ERROR flags errors on

particular source lines, records the error number in 'errs' and following compilation ERRORMSG prints a summary of all errors detected.

ENDSKIP This procedure underlines all those characters which it has been necessary to ignore from the last recorded error position to the current column 'cc'.

ERROR In the event of a compile time error being detected, this procedure is
called to mark the position in the line in which the error was detected, and to
add the error number, which was passed as a parameter, to the set of detected
errors (accessed globally).

FATAL This procedure is called when an attempt is made to insert an item into
a table which is already full. The single parameter, an integer, is used to indicate
the table, a message is printed and the program aborts. Tables are indicated as
follows 1(TAB), 2(BTAB), 3(RCONST), 4(ATAB), 5(DISPLAY), 6(CODE),
7(STAB).

OPTIONS A comment which has the character '$' as its first character is used by
the user to specify options to the compiler. These options take the form of a
letter followed by a plus or minus sign. A list of options separated by commas
may be given. The procedure OPTIONS reads a list of options and uses the procedure SWITCH to change the state of the boolean variable which controls that
option. Note that in the program given here the letter t is used to specify
whether the compiler's symbol table is printed, and the letter s is used to specify
whether the run time stack should be printed on entry to a procedure in the
user's program.

SWITCH The current value 'ch' is inspected to determine whether it is '+', or '−'.
The value true is returned for plus, and false for minus. A character other than
plus or minus causes an error to be flagged. Characters following plus or minus
are ignored until a comma or an asterisk is encountered.

SETUP The arrays KEY, and KSY are very closely related. The reserved word
strings are held in KEY while the element in the set of symbols corresponding
to these strings is held in KSY. If a reserved word is found in position 'i' of
KEY, then the corresponding symbol in the set of symbols is found in KSY[i].
Both arrays are initialised in SETUP. The array SPS having the special characters
(brackets etc) as index, and their symbol names as element values, is also initialised in SETUP.

ENTERIDS This procedure simply consists of twenty nine calls of the procedure
ENTER. The result of these calls is to insert the names of the standard types
and the standard functions made available to the user into TAB (the symbol table).

PRINTTABLES If an appropriate directive is given in the options list of the
user's program this procedure is called to print the contents of the tables TAB
(from position 28 onwards), BTAB, ATAB (if used), and CODE.

10.3.2 Lexical Analysis

NEXTCH This is the most heavily used of all the procedures in the compiler. It is called by INSYMBOL whenever another character is required from the input stream. A line of source input is read character by character and stored in the array 'line'. As each character is read it is also printed to produce the program listing. Before each line of the source the value of 'lc', the pointer into the table CODE, is printed so that the correspondence between lines of source and the instructions in CODE may be seen. Most calls of NEXTCH will result in the next character being extracted from the line buffer and assigned to 'ch'. Before printing a new line of the source listing, a check is made to see whether the previous line attracted any error indicators. If so, a writeln is issued and the error position indicator 'errpos' is reset. As a result of the errors detected it may have been necessary to skip over some of the input characters before the compiler could recover. If this has happened, then the characters which were skipped must be underlined before a new source line is printed. This is also dealt with by NEXTCH.

INSYMBOL Procedure INSYMBOL converts groups of characters into tokens so that the rest of the syntax analysis can be done more easily. INSYMBOL may thus be called a recogniser. Each character or group of characters recognised will cause the global variable 'sy' (used extensively in the program) to take an appropriate value from the enumerated type 'symbol'. Thus if the character ':' is recognised, 'sy' takes the value 'colon'. However if the colon is followed by '=', then 'sy' is assigned the value 'becomes'. The case statement which forms nearly all of the body of INSYMBOL makes it easy to see what happens to single characters or character pairs. It is not so easy to see what happens to symbols starting with a letter or a digit. Following an initial letter, letters and digits are read until a non-alphanumeric character is found. No more than ten characters of the symbol string are stored in 'id'. The supposition is made that this will be a reserved word and accordingly a search is made of the array KEY which holds all such reserved words. If the symbol is located then 'sy' is given the appropriate value from KSY; otherwise 'sy' is given the value 'ident'. Note that the symbol may prove to be one of the standard identifiers.

In the event that our first character was a digit, an attempt is made to recognise a number. An integer constant causes few problems; the constant is evaluated and 'sy' is left as 'intcon'. We note in passing that while checks are made on the value of the constant and the number of digits it comprises, in many implementations these checks will not stop overflow and prevent errors. In the evaluation of what is apparently an integer constant, a decimal point or exponent indicator E may be encountered. Upon encountering '.' it must be ascertained whether it is immediately followed by another '.', if so a range indicator rather than a decimal point has been encountered. If not, 'sy' is given the value 'realcon' and the real constant must be evaluated. The partial sum becomes 'rnum' rather than 'inum'. After the decimal point 'rnum' is multiplied by ten and the new digit added to give a new partial sum. For each such digit, 'e' is decreased by one, having been given the value zero when the decimal point was encountered. When the exponent indicator E is encountered in the input, the procedure READSCALE is called to evaluate the constant which follows. This integer value is added to 'e'. Thus by differing routes we have reached the position where all characters of our real constant have been read and 'rnum' contains a real value computed regardless of the decimal point. The power of ten by which 'rnum' must be multiplied (or divided), in order that it correctly represents the value which was input, is held in 'e'. The procedure ADJUSTSCALE is called so that the multiplying (or dividing) factor represented by 'e' can be computed and used to scale 'rnum'.

INSYMBOL must also identify comments. Most comments will be ignored; however some may contain directives. A check must be made that no directives appear before the comment is ignored. The procedure OPTIONS will identify directives and will, with the help of procedure SWITCH, set boolean variables as required by the directives.

The detection of a string quote causes INSYMBOL to attempt to identify a string. Any string which is recognised is, if legal, entered in STAB and 'sy' is given the value 'string'. If a string is of only one character the value adopted by 'sy' is 'charcon'.

Note that the seven characters $ [@ ? & ↑ ! may not appear in a program processed by Pascal S except in strings.

10.3.3 Syntax Analysis

In attempting to answer the question "does the program being processed satisfy the syntax rules of Pascal?", it would help to use symbols (tokens). Thus frequent use will be made of INSYMBOL. For valid programs we simply proceed from the examination of one construct to the next. It will always be possible to enumerate those symbols which should occur next. However, in the event of a user error, the logical assumptions about what follows the present symbol will be invalid. Accordingly procedures are provided to minimise the effect of such errors by skipping such text as is necessary to enable Pascal S to resume sensible analysis. In all of the procedures associated with syntax analysis considerable use is made of the set of symbols, 'symset', and particular subsets of it. These subsets are:—

constbegsys	[plus,minus,intcon,charcon,ident]
typebegsys	[ident,arraysy,recordsy]
blockbegsys	[constsy,typesy,varsy,procsy,funcsy,beginsy]
facbegsys	[intcon,realcon,charcon,ident,lparent,notsy]
statbegsys	[beginsy,ifsy,whilesy,repeatsy,forsy,casesy]
stantyps	[notyp,ints,reals,bools,chars]

Thus for example, the symbol which starts a block could be one of <u>const</u>, <u>type</u>, <u>var</u>, <u>procedure</u>, <u>function</u> or, if there are no declarations, <u>begin</u>. A test of whether we have one of these symbols is much more easily seen as a test of whether the symbol 'sy' is in the subset 'blockbegsys'. With this in mind it can be seen that passing information about symbols between procedures is conveniently achieved by having a parameter of type 'symset'. Two such procedures, SKIP and TEST, play a key role in preventing our analysis from running into trouble.

SKIP This procedure has two parameters, one of type 'symset', the other an integer which is an error number. After flagging the error, all symbols which are not in the subset of symbols passed as an actual parameter are ignored.

TEST Procedure TEST has two parameters of type 'symset' and a third which is an integer. If the current symbol is not in the subset given by the first parameter, then all those symbols in the subset formed by the union of the first and second parameters are ignored. Normally we would expect that the analysis would proceed in a recursive descent without problems. However at each level in this descent it is important to know which symbols one would need to recognise, in order to recover from a user error. This is achieved by passing to BLOCK such a set of symbols (blockbegsys, statbegsys). In turn BLOCK, when calling procedures at a lower level, will extend this set as appropriate. This information is made available through the formal parameter of BLOCK 'fsys'. The name 'fsys' is used in other procedure declarations, but the role of the corresponding parameter is always the same.

TESTSEMICOLON This procedure checks that the current symbol is a semicolon, in which case the analysis continues. If the symbol is a comma or a colon then an error is flagged and the analysis continues. For any other value of the current symbol we assume that the user's error is gross and procedure TEST is called to locate a suitable reference point from which the analysis can continue.

BLOCK Although this procedure is the largest to be used in the sense that it embraces many other procedures, it is easy to see what it does. When called, it is assumed that the procedure or function name has just been processed and that therefore the current symbol is a left bracket (marking the start of the parameter list), or a colon (as would happen if a function had no parameter list), or a semicolon (in the case of a procedure with no parameter list). It should be noted that the first call of BLOCK, to deal with the user's program body, will be slightly different, since what corresponds to the parameter list will have been processed before the call, and 'sy' will be left pointing at the semicolon which follows.

If appropriate the parameter list is processed, as is the type designator for a function. Thereafter a search is made for the reserved words – const, type, var. If located, procedures are called which will undertake all necessary table entries. If procedure or function declarations follow they are processed. Following these a test is made for a begin symbol. Subsequently the statements forming the program body are processed until the final full stop of the program is found.

CONSTDEC This procedure, which has no parameters, is called following the recognition of the reserved word const. As indicated in the syntax diagrams it expects to find one or more occurrences of an identifier followed by an equals sign, which is followed by a constant value (as recognised by procedure CONSTANT). The recognition of a real constant causes the real value to be entered into the table of reals. In this situation the symbol table entry for the symbol must be made to point to the table of real constants. For other constants the 'adr' field of the symbol table holds the value of the symbol. The procedure terminates when the list of identifiers is exhausted.

TYPEDECLARATION A program or procedure may contain user type definitions following the reserved word type. This procedure, which has no parameters, must process all identifiers defined in this section. An identifier is recognised and added to the symbol table. The equals sign which should follow is then located. A type definition following the equals is processed by procedure TYP. The information produced by the procedure TYP is entered into the symbol table. This processing is repeated for all identifiers defined in the type section.

VARIABLEDECLARATION All identifiers defined following the reserved word var are processed by this procedure. All variables appearing in a list prior to a colon are entered into the symbol table, and a type indicator should follow the colon. This is processed by the procedure TYP. Since all identifiers declared as variables will require storage space on the run time stack, information which will permit reference to the allocated storage cell or cells must be stored in TAB, and the count of local space required by this block must be increased accordingly. This processing must be repeated for all identifier declarations encountered in the var section.

PRODECLARATION This procedure, which has no parameters, is called whenever the reserved words procedure or function are recognised by procedure BLOCK. The procedure or function name is entered into the symbol table. The remainder of the definition is dealt with simply by calling the procedure BLOCK. Since the procedures called by BLOCK to process the executable statements of the body of the user procedure will generate appropriate code for their run time execution, the final action of PROCDECLARATION is to generate the instruction to exit from the procedure or function.

STATEMENT Procedure STATEMENT has one parameter of type 'symset'. This procedure has the task of analysing all executable statements in the program. Its parameter will on any particular call give a set of symbols which can be used in error recovery. If, for example, unexpected symbols are encountered, causing an error to be reported, then symbols from the input stream are ignored until one of those symbols in the set defined by the actual parameter is recognised. Analysis may then continue.

As may be anticipated, STATEMENT identifies the different kinds of statements which may be encountered in a block. A different procedure is used in the analysis of each such statement. The body of STATEMENT can therefore be made very compact and consists of a <u>case</u> statement which uses the first symbol of a statement to select which procedure to call. The least straightforward case is the one in which the first symbol of a statement is a user defined symbol (an identifier). In this case a decision must be made as to whether the statement is an assignment statement, a procedure call, or the assignment to a function identifier. This decision is made by considering the value of the 'obj' field in TAB for the identifier concerned.

CALL As its name implies, this procedure deals with the call of a procedure or function. The procedure has two parameters, one of type 'symset' having the same purpose as outlined for the procedure STATEMENT, the other an integer giving the index in TAB of the procedure/function name. The first action upon encountering a procedure/function call is to generate a *mark stack* instruction. After this, the actual parameter list is processed. Because value parameters may in fact be expressions, the procedure EXPRESSION (described later) is called to generate code which will enable such parameters to be evaluated at run time. The result of this code will be to leave the value of the parameter on the run time stack. In the case of <u>var</u> parameters, what must be put on the stack is not the value of the parameter but a reference to it. Since the actual parameter may be an array element or the field of a record, care must be taken to identify these items and compute and generate an appropriate reference using SELECTOR. When all parameters have been processed (i.e. when the closing round bracket has been reached) and the check on the number of actual parameters has been made, a call of the appropriate procedure can be generated. If this call involves a change of level, then the call of the procedure must be followed by a call to UPDATEDISPLAY. (The role of DISPLAY at run time is discussed in Chapter 11).

EXPRESSION When considering the procedure EXPRESSION, reference should be made to the syntax diagrams for an expression. It will be seen that the definition of expression, simple expression, term and factor are closely related. Not surprisingly the procedure EXPRESSION contains the definition of the procedures SIMPLEEXPRESSION, TERM, FACTOR, and also STANDFCT (for dealing with the calls of standard functions).

Expression has two parameters, one of type 'symset' used as we have seen before for error recovery, and one 'x' of type 'item'. The type of the expression is returned via 'x'. If no boolean operators follow the first simple expression, then the type returned via 'x' is the type obtained from SIMPLEEXPRESSION. When a boolean operator is detected the type of both operands is checked and, if necessary, made the same before code is generated for the comparison. In this case the type boolean is returned via the parameter 'x'.

SIMPLEEXPRESSION A simple expression is a term, or two terms separated by one of the operators plus, minus, or. The procedure has two parameters, one of type 'symset' for error recovery, and one of type 'item' via which the type of the simple expression is returned to the caller. In the body of the procedure, the current symbol is first examined to determine whether it is a monadic operator. If there is a monadic operator, then the following term cannot have type boolean but must have type integer or real. An error (33) is indicated if this is not the case. In the event that a valid unary minus is detected, a negate instruction is generated. If there were no initial operator a call to TERM is made. In any event, having dealt with the first (and possibly only) term of a simple expression the while loop of the procedure body is executed. As long as this loop encounters +, −, or or between valid terms it will continue processing. The result will be in 'x.typ' and a careful check is always kept on types. If these are illegal, an error is indicated; where necessary, RESULTTYPE is called to change the type of results. An or instruction, an add instruction, or a subtract instruction (real or integer), is generated as appropriate.

TERM Like the procedures which immediately enclose it, TERM has two parameters, one of type 'symset' and one of type 'item'. Their functions are the same as in the preceding two procedures.

The operators which separate two factors are multiply, divide (real and integer) modulus and and. The first action of the procedure is to call the procedure FACTOR to deal with the first operand. There follows a while loop which continues processing until something other than one of the operators listed above follows a factor. As we have seen earlier, we need to keep a careful check on the types of operands, giving error indications where necessary and converting types where appropriate. Note that divide has one operator for reals and one for integers. By the time the tests to determine which operator was encountered are made, both factors have been processed; that is, code to evaluate them and leave them on the run time stack has been generated. Thus TERM need only generate the code for that operation which will combine them.

FACTOR This is the innermost of the four principal procedures to process expressions. An examination of the appropriate syntax diagram indicates the form that factors may take. Like its predecessors in this quartet FACTOR has two parameters, one of type 'symset', and one of type 'item'. Their role is the same as that of the parameters of TERM, SIMPLEEXPRESSION, and EXPRESSION.

At its simplest, a factor may be the name of a constant defined either globally or at the head of some enclosing block. If this is the case, an instruction to load it onto the run time stack is generated. If the factor is a variable then more care in its reference must be taken. In the case where the variable is of a standard type, then the load instruction generated need refer only to the level and offset on the stack frame of the required item. If, however, the variable is a record field or an array element, then SELECTOR must be called to resolve the reference. A factor might also be a function call, in which case STANDFCT is called for standard functions, while procedure CALL is invoked for user defined functions.

A factor may also be a manifest constant or a parenthesized expression. A manifest real will be stored in the real constant table and the load instruction generated will refer to the relevant entry in the table. In the case of character or integer constants, versions of the load instructions exist which will load such constants directly. If a parenthesis is located, then, following the call of EX-PRESSION, a check is made that a matching parenthesis exists. If the factor under consideration is <u>not</u> followed by a factor, then a recursive call to FACTOR is made followed by the generation of the logical not instruction. This processing is repeated under control of a <u>while</u> statement.

ASSIGNMENT As its name suggests, this procedure is called by procedure STATEMENT when an assignment statement has been encountered. Before the call of ASSIGNMENT the level and the offset of the item on the left of the assignment statement are obtained from the symbol table, and these are passed to the procedure as its parameters 'lv', 'add' respectively. An instruction is then generated which will put the address of this reference on the run time stack. If the item on the left of the assignment is a record field or an array element, then a call of SELECTOR is made to resolve the reference. Thereafter, procedure EXPRESSION is called to process the right hand side of the assignment. This call will necessarily involve the generation of instructions which will evaluate the expression at run time. Checks are then made on the compatibility of the types of items to the left and right of the assignment. If necessary, an error will be indicated; if appropriate, a type conversion will be generated.

COMPOUNDSTATEMENT A compound statement is a sequence of statements surrounded by <u>begin</u> and <u>end</u>. The procedure has no parameters, and calls STATEMENT a sufficient number of times to process all statements forming the compound statement. An error is given if no terminating <u>end</u> is found.

IFSTATEMENT An <u>if</u> statement may take different forms (with or without an <u>else</u> part) and care must be taken that both are dealt with correctly. An <u>if</u> statement will generate code for the expression following the <u>if</u> and code for the statements following the <u>then</u> and the <u>else</u> (if it is present). These sections of code must be separated by branch instructions, which must be generated at an appropriate point in the generation sequence. However, at the time when the conditional jump between the expression and the statement which follows <u>then</u> is generated, we do not know the location at which the code for the statement following <u>else</u> begins. The branch instruction is generated without a destination field, and its position in CODE is stored in 'lcl'. A call to STATE-MENT processes the statement following <u>then</u> and generates code for it. If the conditional statement has no <u>else</u> part, then the current value of 'lc', which gives the location in CODE of the next instruction to be generated, is used to complete the instruction at position 'lcl' of CODE. When the conditional statement is found to have an <u>else</u> part, the current value of 'lc' is copied to 'lc2', an unconditional branch with no address part is generated, the conditional branch at position 'lcl' is completed by inserting the value of 'lc' and a call to STATEMENT is made. Upon completion of this call the unconditional branch at position 'lc2' of CODE is completed by inserting 'lc' as the destination.

The statement

$$\text{if } a > 10 \text{ then } b := 0 \text{ else } c := 0$$

causes the following code to be generated:

location	operation	operands x	y	action
3	1	1	5	
4	24		10	a > 10
5	49			
6	11		11	branch to 11 if false
7	0	1	6	
8	24		0	b:=0
9	38			
10	10		14	jump to 14
11	0	1	7	
12	24		0	c:=0
13	38			
14				

CASESTATEMENT This procedure has no parameters, but it has two local procedures CASELABEL, and ONECASE. These procedures make use of the two arrays which are local to CASESTATEMENT. The array CASETAB is an array of records where each record contains a label value and the index of the array CODE which the label will reference. The array EXITTAB contains the index in array CODE of the jump instruction which terminates each case. The destination of this jump can only be filled in when the case statement has been completely processed. The local procedures are described before continuing the description of CASESTATEMENT.

CASELABEL Since several labels may prefix one of the statements of a <u>case</u> statement, the procedure CASELABEL is called for each. For each label an entry is made in CASETAB of the label value and the present value of the index into code. Existing entries in CASETAB are checked to ensure that a label is not used more than once. Checks are also included for the type of the label, and that the number of labels does not exceed the implementation defined maximum.

ONECASE This procedure will deal with each entry in the list of possible statements which may be accessed by the selector. The label or labels preceding the colon are dealt with by a call or calls of CASELABEL. After the colon, the procedure STATEMENT is called to deal with what follows. Finally, note is kept in EXITTAB of the index in CODE of the jump instruction which is then generated.

Following the reserved word case will be an expression. This is processed by calling the procedure EXPRESSION. A test is made to check that the type of this expression is allowed before generating the instruction which will jump to the branch table. This branch table follows the last code generated for the statements which make up the case statement. Thereafter each alternative of the case statement is processed by repeated use of ONECASE. The entries in CASETAB are now used to construct the branch table, having one entry for each label used. Finally, the EXITTABLE is used to complete the destination in the jump which is the final instruction in the sequence of instructions generated for each alternative of the case statement.

The case statement

        case valid of
            true : a:=4;
            false : a:=2;
        end

causes the following code to be generated:

location	operation	operands x	y	action
57	1	1	8	load value of 'valid'
58	12		67	find value in case table
59	0	1	5	
60	24		4	a:=4
61	38			
62	10		72	jump exit case statement
63	0	1	5	
64	24		2	a:=2
65	38			
66	10		72	exit case statement

case table starts here

67	13	1	value (true)
68	13	59	destination
69	13	0	value (false)
70	13	63	destination
71	10	0	end of case table
72			

REPEATSTATEMENT Having no parameters, this procedure is called upon locating the reserved word <u>repeat</u>. The index of CODE is stored in 'lcl' and thereafter procedure STATEMENT is used to process the statements occurring before the <u>until</u> which matches <u>repeat</u>. The expression following <u>until</u> is processed. If it is not of type boolean, or a function which will leave a boolean on the top of the run time stack, an error will be signalled. Finally, a conditional jump is generated which will branch back to the start of the loop (or not) according to the value at the top of the run time stack.

The <u>repeat</u> statement

```
repeat
    c:=c-1
until c=0
```

causes the following code to be generated:

location	operation	operands x	y	action
43	0	1	7	
44	1	1	7	
45	24		1	c:=c+1
46	53			
47	38			
48	1	1	7	
49	24		0	c=0
50	45			
51	11		43	jump to 43 if false
52				

WHILESTATEMENT This procedure, which has no parameters, is called after the reserved word <u>while</u> has been recognised. The current position in CODE is stored in 'lcl' and the expression following the <u>while</u> is processed. If the expression is not boolean or a function which can produce a boolean result, then an error is flagged. The current index into CODE is stored before generating an incomplete branch which will ultimately branch round the body of the while statement. Following the recognition of the symbol do, procedure STATEMENT is called to process the body of the while statement. An unconditional branch instruction is now generated. The destination part of this branch is obtained from 'lcl', thus completing the loop back to the controlling expression. Finally the conditional jump preceding the body of the while statement is completed with the current value of the index to CODE.

The while statement

$$\text{while } b < 10 \text{ do } b := b + 1$$

causes the following code to be generated

location	operation	operands x	y	action
→30	1	1	6	b<10
31	24		10	
32	47			
33	11		40	exit if false
34	0	1	6	
35	1	1	6	b:=b+1
36	24		1	
37	52			
38	38			
39	10		30	jump to location 30
40				

FORSTATEMENT This procedure will be called following recognition of the reserved word for. An identifier should of course follow. If this identifier is not in the identifier table then it is assumed to be of type integer, and processing is allowed to continue without generating an 'undeclared identifier' message! More normally, the identifier will be in TAB and should be flagged as a 'vvariable'. If this is so, an instruction to load its address on the stack is generated. A check is then made that the variable has a suitable type and error messages are reported as appropriate. The symbol ':=' should be recognised followed by an expression (the initial value of the controlled variable), which should have the same type as the controlled variable. Thereafter follows the reserved word to, (or downto), which in turn is followed by a further expression, the upper (or lower) limit. At this point the first of the special pair of for statement control instructions is generated. Each of these instructions has a destination (reference into CODE) as its operand. The first of the for loop control instructions compares the initial value for the controlled variable with the final value, in order to establish whether the for statement should be executed at all. If not, a branch to the statement which follows the for statement is made. Since, at the time the first loop control instruction is generated, the destination of the branch is not known, the position of the instruction in CODE is kept in 'lcl'. The first loop control instruction is followed by the instructions of the <u>for</u> statement body. The position of the first of these instructions is kept in 'lc2' and, following the call of STATEMENT which processes the <u>for</u> statement body, the second of the <u>for</u> statement control instructions is generated. This has as its destination the instruction indicated by 'lc2'. Since the next instruction to be generated is the first instruction of the statement which follows the <u>for</u> statement, the partial instruction indicated by 'lcl' is completed. The work of FORSTATEMENT is now finished.

The <u>for</u> statement

$$\text{\underline{for} } a := 1 \text{ \underline{to} } 10 \text{ \underline{do} } c := c + 1$$

causes the following code to be generated:

location	operation	operands x	y	action
17	0	1	5	load address of 'a'
18	24		1	load initial value
19	24		10	load final value
20	14		27	exit if limits violated
21	0	1	7	
22	1	1	7	
23	24		1	c := c + 1
24	52			
25	38			
26	15		21	jump to 21 if not finished
27				

STANDPROC Procedure STANDPROC deals with the standard input/output procedures read, readln, write, writeln. The procedure has one parameter which identifies the standard procedures listed as 1,2,3,4 respectively. For read, readln, a check is made that the actual parameter list is properly formed. Each parameter must be a variable and if a parameter is a record field or an array element, procedure SELECTOR is called to produce the appropriate referencing information. Instructions are generated to ensure that the address of the variable is placed on the run time stack followed by a read instruction. If the standard function is readln, a readln instruction would be the final instruction generated.

In dealing with the parameters of the output procedures, checks are made to see that the parameter lists are well formed. If the parameter is a string, instructions must be generated to put its length on the stack, followed by the instruction to write a string which will contain the reference to the string table. Any other parameter may be of the type ⟨expression⟩:⟨expression⟩ and these items are recognised and processed by using the procedure EXPRESSION. Instructions are generated as appropriate to write a real with given field widths (remember two colons can be used in the field specification of reals) and to write other items to a given field width or to default field widths. If the output procedure is writeln, a writeln instruction is generated.

10.3.4 Semantic Routines
These are divided into two types:

i) those declared outside the procedure BLOCK:
READSCALE INSYMBOL calls READSCALE when the exponent symbol 'E' is discovered in a number. READSCALE reads the characters which follow 'E' until the non digit which follows the exponent is encountered. As the digits of the exponent are found, the value of the exponent is accumulated.

ADJUSTSCALE This is called by INSYMBOL to scale a floating point number. The procedure INSYMBOL forms the mantissa of a floating point number in 'rnum' and READSCALE produces the value of the exponent 'e'. By repeatedly dividing the exponent by two and squaring the value of a variable having initial value 10, the value of the exponent as a multiplier or divisor is obtained. The mantissa 'rnum' is then multiplied or divided, according to whether the exponent was positive or negative.

ENTER Procedure ENTER is used in the initialisation phase to enter the standard identifiers into the symbol table TAB. This table and its pointer 't' are global to the procedure.

ENTERARRAY This procedure has three parameters representing the index type, the lower bound and the upper bound of an array. As each index is processed in the array declaration, this procedure will be called to enter the index information. Note that upon each call (i.e. for each subscript) a new entry is created in ATAB.

ENTERBLOCK A new entry in BTAB is created and the references to the last variable declared at this level to zero. The pointer to the last parameter is also zeroed, since when this procedure is called the parameters have not yet been processed.

ENTERREAL Before creating a new entry in RCONST the procedure checks the existing contents for an identical constant to the one about to be inserted. If such a constant exists then reference is made to it, otherwise a new entry is created.

ii) those declared within the procedure BLOCK
ENTER This procedure is responsible for adding user symbols to the symbol table TAB. Before making an entry it is necessary to check that no other entry

of a similar name exists. This check is made by entering the new name at position zero in the table, and then making a search from the last entry $'t'$. This search should result in a match being found at subscript zero. If this is not the case then the identifier already exists (subscript > 0). If the identifier is found to be unique, a new entry is made in TAB. As well as entering the name the procedure enters the $'mode'$ of the identifier (the role it adopts). Both items are provided as parameters.

LOC An identifier (passed as parameter) is located in the symbol table. This must be done without violating the scope rules governing the identifier's usage. In order to do this, the identifier is inserted at position zero, then using DISPLAY and BTAB to identify the start of the identifier chains in the current and enclosing blocks, a search is made of the relevant parts of TAB. If the identifier is located, its position in TAB is assigned to LOC. If no accessible identifier of that name is located, a suitable error is flagged.

ENTERVARIABLE A check is made that the current symbol is an identifier before entering it as a $'variable'$ using ENTER.

CONSTANT This procedure has two parameters and is called whenever a constant is expected in the source text — for example in the declaration of array bounds. Allowable constants are character constants, real constants and constant identifiers. The first of the two parameters of the procedure is a set of symbols which mark the termination of the constant. The second is a variable of type $'conrec'$ and is used to communicate the type and the value of the constant discovered.

TYP In the declaration of any variable, there is, following the colon, a type field. This may be a standard type, a user defined type, or it may be an array or record definition. The procedure TYP is called after the discovery of the colon. It has four formal parameters, a set of delimiters $'fsys'$, a variable to indicate the type of the object scanned and two integers $'rf'$, $'sz'$. In the event that the type is already entered in TAB, $'rf'$ is assigned the ref value of the appropriate entry (either zero, a pointer to ATAB or a pointer to BTAB) while $'sz'$ in the case of arrays and records is given the value of their size.

If the symbol which follows the colon is not a simple identifier but an array or record definition, then the information referred to above must be computed rather than simply copied from TAB. For arrays this is achieved by calling the procedure ARRAYTYP. For records the processing is carried out in TYP; all field identifiers are entered into TAB and, following the colon for each field designator, a recursive call is made to TYP.

ARRAYTYP Two formal parameters are used by this procedure to communicate to its caller the appropriate ATAB index $'ref'$ and the number of storage units required $'sz'$. When ARRAYTYP is called it is assumed that the lower bound is about to be processed. Bounds of the array are evaluated and entered into ATAB and the size of the vector computed. Since an array can be multi-dimensional, it may be considered a vector or vectors. The procedure ARRAY-TYP is recursive to enable it to deal with this. Information about the size, bounds, and subscript type of each vector is entered into ATAB. The outermost entry in ATAB for any array gives the size of the whole array.

PARAMETERLIST This procedure has no parameters and is called to process the formal parameter list of a procedure. The name of each parameter must be entered into TAB, together with information indicating whether it is a variable or a value parameter, its type (a type identifier must be given in a parameter list), its size (one storage unit for variable parameters) and its offset in the procedure stack frame.

SELECTOR This procedure has one parameter of type 'symset', with the same role as that described for procedure STATEMENT, and another 'v' of type 'item'. In the procedure body, values will be assigned to 'v.typ' and 'v.ref'. SELECTOR has the responsibility for dealing with items which cannot be referred to by a simple symbol name. Thus it takes care of references to the fields of records and references to the subscripts of arrays. The procedure will be called after recognition of the record name or the array name, and 'sy' at this point will be either the fullstop which separates a record name from its field name, or the square bracket which separates an array name from the subscript list. The procedure must determine from appropriate tables the type 'v.typ' of the field or array element and its offset from the start of the field or record 'v.ref'. In each case code is generated to effect this reference. It should be noted that in the case of an array element there may be several subscripts to evaluate before reference is complete. Because a record may contain a record (or an array), and an array may have an array element as its subscript, the work of SELECTOR is not complete until the symbol following the field identifier is other than a fullstop or a left bracket.

CALL As its name implies, this procedure deals with the call of a procedure or function. The procedure has two parameters, one of type 'symset' having the same purpose as outlined for the procedure STATEMENT, the other an integer giving the index in TAB of the procedure/function name. The first action taken upon encountering a procedure/function call is to generate a "mark stack" instruction. Following this, the actual parameter list is processed. Because value parameters may in fact be expressions, the procedure EXPRESSION is called to generate code which will enable such parameters to be evaluated at run time. The result of this code will be to leave the value of the parameter on the run time stack. In the case of var parameters, what must be put on the stack is not the value of the parameter but a reference to the parameter. Since the actual parameter may be an array element or the field of a record, care must be taken to identify these items and compute and generate an appropriate reference using SELECTOR. When all parameters have been processed (i.e. when the closing round bracket has been reached, and the check on the number of actual parameters has been made) a call of the appropriate procedure can be generated. If this call involves a change of level, then the call of the procedure must be followed by a call to UPDATEDISPLAY.

RESULTTYPE This function has two parameters. The two parameters and the function have the same type which is 'types'. In practice they will only take the value 'notype', 'ints', or 'reals'. The purpose of the procedure is to check the types of two operands (passed as parameters) and, in the event that one is real and one is integer, a float operation is generated for the integer operand, so that both operands and the result have type real.

STANDFCT STANDFCT is local to the procedure TERM and has one integer parameter 'n'. The value which is passed via 'n' to the procedure is a position in TAB (the symbol table) of the standard function name. Some idea of the ordering of the standard functions in TAB can be gained by examining the procedure ENTERIDS. For most of the standard functions it is simply necessary to evaluate the actual parameter (by calling expression) and to examine the type of result. If the type of the actual parameter is inappropriate for the function, an error is flagged. Where necessary the type is changed by generating a float instruction, otherwise the call of the standard function is generated.

10.3.5 Code Generation
The three procedures below insert instruction codes into the array CODE after checking that there is sufficient room.

EMIT1 inserts an instruction having one operand in CODE. Instructions 8 to 30 have a single operand.

EMIT2 inserts an instruction having two operands into CODE. Instructions 0, 1, 2, 3 have two operands. Except in the case of code 3, these operands represent the level number (x) and offset (y) of an item on the stack.

```
{$g+  }
program pascals(input,output,prd,prr);

{ author: N.Wirth, E.T.H. CH-8092 Zurich, 1.3.76 }

{ modified by R.E.Berry
                Department of Computer Studies
                University of Lancaster

                variants of this program are used on
                Data General Nova, Apple, and
                Western Digital Microengine machines. }


const   nkw  =   27;        { no. of key words }
        alng =   10;        { no. of significant chars in identifiers }
        llng =  121;        { input line length }
        emax =  322;        { max exponent of real numbers }
        emin =-292;         { min exponent }
        kmax =   15;        { max no. of significant digits }
        tmax =  100;        { size of table }
        bmax =   20;        { size of block-table }
        amax =   30;        { size of array-table }
        c2max=   20;        { size of real constant table }
        csmax=   30;        { max no. of cases }
        cmax =  800;        { size of code  }
        lmax =    7;        { maximum level }
        smax =  600;        { size of string-table }
        ermax =  58;        { max error no. }
        omax =   63;        { highest order code }
        xmax = 32767;       { 2**8 - 1 }
        nmax = 32767;       { 2**8 - 1 }

        lineleng  =  132;  { output line length }
        linelimit =  200;
        stacksize = 1450;

type symbol = (intcon,realcon,charcon,stringcon,
               notsy,plus,minus,times,idiv,rdiv,imod,andsy,orsy,
               eql,neq,gtr,geq,lss,leq,
               lparent,rparent,lbrack,rbrack,comma,semicolon,period,
               colon,becomes,constsy,typesy,varsy,funcsy,
               procsy,arraysy,recordsy,programsy,ident,
               beginsy,ifsy,casesy,repeatsy,whilesy,forsy,
               endsy,elsesy,untilsy,ofsy,dosy,tosy,downtosy,thensy);

     index  = -xmax .. +xmax;
     alfa   = packed array [1..alng] of char;
     object = (konstant,vvariable,type1,prozedure,funktion);
     types  = (notyp,ints,reals,bools,chars,arrays,records);
     symset = set of symbol;
     typset = set of types;
     item   = record
                  typ: types; ref: index
              end ;
     order  = packed record
                  f: -omax..+omax;
                  x: -lmax..+lmax;
                  y: -nmax..+nmax
              end ;

var ch    : char;                { last character read from source program }
    rnum  : real;                { real number from insymbol }
    i,j   : integer;
    inum  : integer;             { integer from insymbol }
    sleng : integer;             { string length }
    cc    : integer;             { character counter }
    lc    : integer;             { program location counter }
    ll    : integer;             { length of current line }
    errpos: integer;
    t,a,b,sx,c1,c2: integer;     { indices to tables }
```

```
    iflag, oflag, skipflag,
        stackdump, prtables : boolean;

    sy      : symbol;              { last symbol read by insymbol }
    errs    : set of 0..ermax;
    id      : alfa;               { identifier from insymbol }
    progname: alfa;
    stantyps: typset;
    constbegsys,typebegsys,blockbegsys,facbegsys,statbegsys: symset;

    line        : array [1..llng] of char;
    objectcode  : array [1 .. 5] of char;
    typescode   : array [1 .. 7] of char;
    key         : array [1..nkw] of alfa;
    ksy         : array [1..nkw] of symbol;
    sps         : array [char] of symbol;      { special symbols }
    display     : array [0 .. lmax] of integer;


    tab:        array [0 .. tmax] of       { identifier table }
                packed record
                    name: alfa;            link: index;
                    obj : object;          typ: types;
                    ref : index;        normal: boolean;
                    lev : 0 .. lmax;       adr: integer
                    end ;

    atab:       array [1 .. amax] of       { array-table }
                packed record
                    inxtyp, eltyp: types;
                    elref, low, high, elsize, size: index
                    end ;

    btab:       array [1 .. bmax] of       { block-table }
                packed record
                    last, lastpar, psize, vsize: index
                    end ;

    stab  :     packed array [0..smax] of char;  { string table }
    rconst:     array [1 .. c2max] of real;
    code  :     array [0 .. cmax] of order;

    psin, psout, prr, prd: text;       { default in pascal p }
    inf, outf: string;

procedure errormsg;

var    k: integer;
       msg: array [0..ermax] of alfa;
begin
    msg[ 0] := 'undef id  '; msg[ 1] := 'multi def ';
    msg[ 2] := 'identifier'; msg[ 3] := 'program   ';
    msg[ 4] := ')         '; msg[ 5] := ':         ';
    msg[ 6] := 'syntax    '; msg[ 7] := 'ident, var';
    msg[ 8] := 'of        '; msg[ 9] := '(         ';
    msg[10] := 'id, array '; msg[11] := '[         ';
    msg[12] := ']         '; msg[13] := '..        ';
    msg[14] := ';         '; msg[15] := 'func. type';
    msg[16] := '=         '; msg[17] := 'boolean   ';
    msg[18] := 'convar typ'; msg[19] := 'type      ';
    msg[20] := 'prog.param'; msg[21] := 'too big   ';
    msg[22] := '.         '; msg[23] := 'typ (case)';
    msg[24] := 'character '; msg[25] := 'const id  ';
    msg[26] := 'index type'; msg[27] := 'indexbound';
    msg[28] := 'no array  '; msg[29] := 'type id   ';
    msg[30] := 'undef type'; msg[31] := 'no record ';
    msg[32] := 'boole type'; msg[33] := 'arith type';
    msg[34] := 'integer   '; msg[35] := 'types     ';
    msg[36] := 'param type'; msg[37] := 'variab id ';
    msg[38] := 'string    '; msg[39] := 'no.of pars';
    msg[40] := 'real numbr'; msg[41] := 'type      ';
```

```
  msg[42] := 'real type '; msg[43] := 'integer    ';
  msg[44] := 'var, const'; msg[45] := 'var, proc ';
  msg[46] := 'types (:=)'; msg[47] := 'typ (case)';
  msg[48] := 'type      '; msg[49] := 'store ovfl';
  msg[50] := 'constant  '; msg[51] := ':=        ';
  msg[52] := 'then      '; msg[53] := 'until     ';
  msg[54] := 'do        '; msg[55] := 'to downto ';
  msg[56] := 'begin     '; msg[57] := 'end       ';
  msg[58] := 'factor    ';

  writeln(psout); writeln(psout,' key words');
  k:=0;
  while errs <> [] do
  begin
    while not (k in errs) do k := k+1;
    writeln(psout,k,'  ',msg[k]);
    errs := errs - [k]
  end {while errs}
end { errormsg } ;

procedure endskip;

begin                 { underline skipped part of input }
  while errpos < cc do
  begin
    write(psout,'-'); errpos := errpos + 1
  end ;
  skipflag := false
end { endskip } ;

procedure nextch;   { read next character; process line end }

begin
  if cc = 11
  then begin
    if eof(psin)
    then begin
      writeln(psout);
      writeln(psout,' program incomplete');
      errormsg;
      exit(pascals); { abort in ucsd system }
    end ;
    if errpos <> 0
    then begin
      if skipflag then endskip;
      writeln(psout);
      errpos := 0
    end ;
    write(psout,lc:5, '   ');
    11 := 0; cc := 0;
    while not eoln(psin) do
    begin
      11 := 11+1;
      read(psin,ch); write(psout,ch);
      line[11] := ch
    end ;
    11 := 11+1;
    read(psin,line[11]); writeln(psout);
  end ;
  cc := cc+1; ch := line[cc];
end { nextch } ;

procedure error(n: integer);

begin
  if errpos = 0 then write(psout,' ****');
  if cc > errpos
  then begin
    write(psout,' ': cc-errpos, '^', n:2);
    errpos := cc+3; errs := errs + [n]
  end
end { error } ;
```

```pascal
procedure fatal(n: integer);

var     msg: array [1..7] of alfa;
begin
  writeln(psout); errormsg;

  msg[ 1] := 'identifier'; msg[ 2] := 'procedures';
  msg[ 3] := 'reals      '; msg[ 4] := 'arrays     ';
  msg[ 5] := 'levels     '; msg[ 6] := 'code       ';
  msg[ 7] := 'strings    ';

  writeln(psout,' compiler table for ', msg[n], ' is too small');
  exit(pascals)    { terminate compilation }
end { fatal } ;


procedure insymbol;                    { reads next symbol }

label  1,2,3 ;
var    i,j,k,e: integer;

  procedure readscale;

  var    s, sign: integer;
  begin
    nextch;
    sign := 1; s := 0;
    if ch = '+'
    then nextch
    else if ch = '-'
          then begin
            nextch; sign := -1
          end ;
    if not ((ch>='0') and (ch<='9'))
    then error(40)
    else repeat
        s := 10*s + ord(ch)-ord('0');
        nextch
      until not ((ch>='0') and (ch<='9'));
    e := s*sign + e
  end { readscale } ;

  procedure adjustscale;

  var    s : integer;
         d,t: real;
  begin
    if k+e > emax
    then error(21)
    else if k+e < emin
          then rnum := 0
          else begin
            s := abs(e); t := 1.0; d := 10.0;
            repeat
              while not odd(s) do
              begin
                s := s div 2; d := sqr(d)
              end ;
              s := s-1; t := d*t
            until s = 0;

            if e >= 0
            then rnum := rnum*t
            else rnum := rnum/t
          end
  end { adjustscale } ;

  procedure options;

    procedure switch(var b:boolean);
```

```
begin
  b:=ch='+';
  if not b
  then if not (ch='-')
          then begin            {  print error message  }
                 while (ch<>'*') and (ch<>',') do nextch;
               end
               else nextch
       else nextch
  end { switch } ;

  begin         {options}
    repeat
      nextch;
      if ch<>'*'
      then begin
        if ch='t'
        then begin
          nextch; switch(prtables)
        end else if ch='s'
                  then begin
                    nextch; switch(stackdump)
                  end;
      end
    until ch<>','
  end  { options } ;

 begin     { insymbol }

1: while ch = ' ' do nextch;

   case ch of
'a','b','c','d','e','f','g','h','i',
'j','k','l','m','n','o','p','q','r',
's','t','u','v','w','x','y','z' :
     begin { identifier or wordsymbol }
       k := 0; id := '          ';
       repeat
         if k < alng
         then begin
           k := k+1; id[k] := ch
         end ;
         nextch
       until not (((ch>='a') and (ch<='z')) or ((ch>='0') and (ch<='9')));

       i := 1; j := nkw;   { binary search }
       repeat
         k := (i+j) div 2;
         if id <= key[k] then j := k-1;
         if id >= key[k] then i := k+1
       until i > j;
       if i-1 > j then sy := ksy[k] else sy := ident
     end;

'0','1','2','3','4','5','6','7','8','9':
     begin { number }
       k := 0; inum := 0; sy := intcon;
       repeat
         inum := inum*10 + ord(ch) - ord('0');
         k := k+1;
         nextch
       until not ((ch>='0') and (ch<='9'));

       if (k > kmax) or (inum > nmax)
       then begin
         error(21); inum := 0; k := 0
       end ;
       if ch = '.'
       then begin
         nextch;
         if ch = '.'
```

[handwritten margin notes:] Ident not entered in Table. Sem A does that

[handwritten margin note:] length max.

[handwritten margin note:] assumes it is a Int constant

[handwritten margin notes:] Decimal part - Returns ⊕   1 .. 10

```
         then ch := ':'
         else begin
           sy := realcon; rnum := inum; e := 0;
           while (ch>='0') and (ch<='9') do
           begin
             e := e-1;
             rnum := 10.0*rnum + (ord(ch)-ord('0'));
             nextch
           end ;
           if e = 0 then error(40);
           if ch = 'e' then readscale;
           if e <> 0 then adjustscale
         end
       end else
         if ch = 'e'
         then begin
           sy := realcon; rnum := inum; e := 0;
           readscale;
           if e <> 0 then adjustscale
         end ;
     end;

 ':':
       begin
         nextch;
         if ch = '='
         then begin
           sy := becomes; nextch
         end else sy := colon
       end ;

 '<' :
       begin
         nextch;
         if ch = '='
         then begin
           sy := leq; nextch
         end else
           if ch = '>'
           then begin
             sy := neq; nextch
           end else sy := lss
       end ;

 '>' :
       begin
         nextch;
         if ch = '='
         then begin
           sy := geq; nextch
         end else sy := gtr
       end ;

 '.' :
       begin
         nextch;
         if ch = '.'
         then begin
           sy := colon; nextch
         end else sy := period
       end ;

 '''' :
       begin
         k := 0;
 2:      nextch;
         if ch = ''''
         then begin
           nextch;
           if ch <> '''' then goto 3
```

begin (* "=" |'<>'| < *) ... end.

```
          end ;
          if sx+k = smax then fatal(7);
          stab[sx+k] := ch; k := k+1;
          if cc = 1
          then begin { end of line }
            k := 0;
          end else goto 2;

  3:      if k = 1
          then begin
            sy := charcon; inum := ord(stab[sx])
          end else if k = 0
                    then begin
                      error(38); sy := charcon; inum := 0
                    end else begin
                      sy := stringcon; inum := sx;
                      sleng := k; sx := sx+k
                    end
        end ;

'(' :
        begin
          nextch;
          if ch <> '*'
          then sy := lparent
          else begin { comment }
            nextch;
            if ch='$' then options;
            repeat
              while ch <> '*' do nextch;
              nextch
            until ch = ')';
            nextch; goto 1
          end
        end ;

'+', '-', '*', '/', ')', '=', ',', '[', ']', ';' :
        begin
          sy := sps[ch]; nextch
        end ;

'$','"','@','?','&','^','!' :      ⟵
        begin
          error(24); nextch; goto 1
        end

      end {case}
end { insymbol } ;

      procedure enter(x0: alfa;  x1: object;
                      x2: types; x3: integer);

      begin
        t := t+1;              { enter standard identifier }
        with tab[t] do
        begin
          name := x0; link := t-1; obj := x1;
          typ := x2; ref := 0; normal := true;
          lev := 0; adr := x3
        end
      end { enter } ;

      procedure enterarray(tp: types; l,h: integer);

      begin
        if l > h then error(27);
        if (abs(l)>xmax) or (abs(h)>xmax)
        then begin
          error(27); l := 0; h := 0;
```

an otherwise clause?

```
    end ;
    if  a = amax
    then fatal(4)
    else begin
      a := a+1;
      with atab[a] do
      begin
        inxtyp := tp; low := 1; high := h
      end
    end
  end { enterarray } ;

  procedure enterblock;

  begin
    if  b = bmax
    then fatal(2)
    else begin
      b := b+1; btab[b].last := 0; btab[b].lastpar := 0
    end
  end { enterblock } ;

  procedure enterreal(x: real);

  begin
    if  c2 = c2max-1
    then fatal(3)
    else begin
      rconst[c2+1] := x; c1 := 1;
      while rconst[c1] <> x do  c1 := c1+1;
      if  c1 > c2 then c2 := c1
    end
  end { enterreal } ;

  procedure emit(fct: integer);

  begin
    if  lc = cmax then fatal(6);
    code[lc].f := fct; lc := lc+1
  end { emit } ;

  procedure emit1(fct,b: integer);

  begin
    if  lc = cmax then fatal(6);
    with code[lc] do
    begin
      f := fct; y := b
    end ;
    lc := lc+1
  end { emit1 } ;

  procedure emit2(fct,a,b: integer);

  begin
    if  lc = cmax then fatal(6);
    with code[lc] do
    begin
      f := fct; x := a; y := b
    end ;
    lc := lc+1
  end { emit2 } ;


  procedure printtables;

  var    i: integer;
         o: order;
```

```
begin
  writeln(psout); writeln(psout); writeln(psout);
  writeln(psout,'   identifiers link  obj  typ  ref   nrm  lev  adr');
  writeln(psout);
  for i := btab[1].last to t do
    with tab[i] do
      writeln(psout,i,'  ',name,link:5, ord(obj):5, ord(typ):5, ref:5,
              ord(normal):5, lev:5, adr:5);

  writeln(psout); writeln(psout); writeln(psout);
  writeln(psout,'blocks     last lpar psze vsze');
  writeln(psout);
  for i := 1 to b do
    with btab[i] do
      writeln(psout,i:4, last:9, lastpar:5, psize:5, vsize:5);

  writeln(psout); writeln(psout); writeln(psout);
  writeln(psout,'arrays    xtyp etyp eref  low high elsz size');
  writeln(psout);

  for i := 1 to a do
    with atab[i] do
      writeln(psout,i:4, ord(inxtyp):9, ord(eltyp):5,
              elref:5, low:5, high:5, elsize:5, size:5);

  writeln(psout); writeln(psout); writeln(psout);
  writeln(psout,' code:'); writeln(psout);

  for i:=0 to lc-1 do
  begin
    write(psout); write(psout,i:5);
    o := code[i]; write(psout,o.f:5);
    if o.f <31
    then if o.f<4
         then write(psout,o.x:2, o.y:5)
         else write(psout,o.y:7)
    else write(psout,'         ');
    writeln(psout,',')
  end;
  writeln(psout);
  writeln(psout,'Starting address is ',tab[btab[1].last].adr:5)

  end { printtables };

procedure block(fsys: symset; isfun: boolean; level: integer);

type   conrec = record case tp: types of
                       ints,chars,bools: (i: integer);
                       reals: (r: real)
                end ;
var    dx : integer;      { data allocation index }
       prt: integer;      { t-index of this procedure }
       prb: integer;      { b-index of this procedure }
       x  : integer;

  procedure skip(fsys: symset; n: integer);

  begin
    error(n); skipflag := true;
    while not (sy in fsys) do insymbol;
    if skipflag then endskip
  end { skip } ;

  procedure test(s1,s2: symset; n: integer);

  begin
    if not (sy in s1) then skip(s1+s2,n)
  end { test } ;

  procedure testsemicolon;
```

```
begin
  if sy = semicolon
  then insymbol
  else begin
    error(14);
    if sy in [comma,colon] then insymbol
  end ;
  test([ident]+blockbegsys., fsys, 6)
end { testsemicolon } ;

procedure enter(id: alfa; k: object);

var    j,l: integer;
begin
  if t = tmax
  then fatal(1)
  else begin
    tab[0].name := id;
    j := btab[display[level]].last;  l := j;
    while tab[j].name <> id do  j := tab[j].link;
    if j <> 0
    then error(1)
    else begin
      t := t+1;
      with tab[t] do
      begin
        name:= id;   link := l;
        obj := k;        typ := notyp;    ref := 0;
        lev := level; adr := 0
      end ;
      btab[display[level]].last := t
    end
  end
end { enter } ;

function loc(id: alfa): integer;

var    i,j: integer;       { locate id in table }
begin
  i := level; tab[0].name := id;    { sentinel }
  repeat
    j := btab[display[i]].last;
    while tab[j].name <> id do  j := tab[j].link;
    i := i-1;
  until (i<0) or (j<>0);
  if j = 0 then error(0);
  loc := j
end { loc } ;

procedure entervariable;

begin
  if sy = ident
  then begin
    enter(id,vvariable); insymbol
  end else error(2)
end { entervariable } ;

procedure constant(fsys: symset; var c: conrec);

var    x, sign: integer;
begin
  c.tp := notyp; c.i := 0;
  test(constbegsys, fsys, 50);
  if sy in constbegsys
  then begin
    if sy = charcon
    then begin
      c.tp := chars; c.i := inum;
      insymbol
```

```
      end else begin
        sign := 1;
        if sy in [plus,minus]
        then begin
          if sy = minus then sign := -1;
          insymbol
        end ;
        if sy = ident
        then begin
          x := loc(id);
          if x <> 0
          then if tab[x].obj <> konstant
                then error(25)
                else begin
                  c.tp := tab[x].typ;
                  if c.tp = reals
                  then c.r := sign*rconst[tab[x].adr]
                  else c.i := sign*tab[x].adr
                end ;
          insymbol
        end else if sy = intcon
                then begin
                  c.tp := ints; c.i := sign*inum;
                  insymbol
                end else if sy = realcon
                        then begin
                          c.tp := reals; c.r := sign*rnum;
                          insymbol
                        end else skip(fsys,50)
      end;
      test(fsys, [], 6)
  end
end { constant } ;

procedure typ(fsys: symset; var tp: types; var rf, sz: integer);

var    eltp    : types;
       elrf, x: integer;
       elsz, offset, t0,t1: integer;

  procedure arraytyp(var aref,arsz: integer);

  var    eltp: types;
         low, high: conrec;
         elrf, elsz: integer;
  begin
    constant([colon,rbrack,rparent,ofsy]+fsys, low);
    if low.tp = reals
    then begin
      error(27);
      low.tp := ints; low.i := 0
    end ;
    if sy = colon then insymbol else error(13);
    constant([rbrack,comma,rparent,ofsy]+fsys, high);
    if high.tp <> low.tp
    then begin
      error(27); high.i := low.i
    end ;
    enterarray(low.tp, low.i, high.i);
    aref := a;
    if sy = comma
    then begin
      insymbol;
      eltp := arrays;
      arraytyp(elrf,elsz)
    end else begin
      if sy = rbrack
      then insymbol
```

```
        else begin
          error(12);
          if sy = rparent then insymbol
        end ;
        if sy = ofsy then insymbol else error(8);
        typ(fsys,eltp,elrf,elsz)
      end ;

      with atab[aref] do
      begin
        arsz := (high-low+1)*elsz; size := arsz;
        eltyp := eltp; elref := elrf; elsize := elsz
      end ;
    end { arraytyp } ;

begin  { typ }
  tp := notyp; rf := 0; sz := 0;
  test(typebegsys, fsys, 10);
  if sy in typebegsys
  then begin
    if sy = ident
    then begin
      x := loc(id);
      if x <> 0
      then with tab[x] do
             if obj <> typel
             then error(29)
             else begin
               tp := typ; rf := ref; sz := adr;
               if tp = notyp then error(30)
             end ;
      insymbol
    end else if sy = arraysy
         then begin
                insymbol;
                if sy = lbrack
                then insymbol
                else begin
                  error(11);
                  if sy = lparent
                  then insymbol
                end ;
                tp := arrays; arraytyp(rf,sz)
              end else begin  { records }
                insymbol;
                enterblock;
                tp := records; rf := b;
                if level = lmax then fatal(5);
                level := level+1; display[level] := b; offset := 0;
                while not (sy in fsys-[semicolon,comma,ident]+[endsy]) do
                begin  { field section }
                  if sy = ident
                  then begin
                    t0 := t; entervariable;
                    while sy = comma do
                    begin
                      insymbol; entervariable
                    end ;
                    if sy = colon then insymbol else error(5);
                    t1 := t;
                    typ(fsys+[semicolon,endsy,comma,ident],eltp,elrf,elsz);
                    while t0 < t1 do
                    begin
                      t0 := t0+1;
                      with tab[t0] do
                      begin
                        typ := eltp;
                        ref := elrf;   normal := true;
                        adr := offset; offset := offset + elsz
                      end
                    end
                  end ; {sy = ident}
```

```
                     if sy <> endsy
                     then begin
                          if sy = semicolon
                          then insymbol
                          else begin
                             error(14);
                             if sy = comma then insymbol
                          end ;
                          test([ident,endsy,semicolon], fsys, 6)
                        end
                     end ; {field section}

                     btab[rf].vsize := offset; sz := offset;
                     btab[rf].psize := 0;
                     insymbol; level := level-1
                  end ; {records}

        test(fsys, [], 6)
     end
end { typ } ;

procedure parameterlist;        { formal parameter list }

var     tp     : types;
        valpar: boolean;
        rf, sz, x, t0: integer;
begin
  insymbol;
  tp := notyp; rf := 0; sz := 0;
  test([ident, varsy], fsys+[rparent], 7);
  while sy in [ident,varsy] do
  begin
    if sy <> varsy
    then valpar := true
    else begin
      insymbol;
      valpar := false
    end ;
    t0 := t; entervariable;
    while sy = comma do
    begin
      insymbol; entervariable;
    end ;
    if sy = colon
    then begin
      insymbol;
      if sy <> ident
      then error(2)
      else  begin
        x := loc(id); insymbol;
        if x <> 0
        then with tab[x] do
             if obj <> type1
             then error(29)
             else begin
               tp := typ;    rf := ref;
               if valpar then sz := adr else sz := 1
             end ;
      end ;
      test([semicolon,rparent], [comma,ident]+fsys, 14)
    end else error(5);
    while t0 < t do
    begin
      t0 := t0+1;
      with tab[t0] do
      begin
        typ := tp; ref := rf;
        adr := dx; lev := level;
        normal := valpar;
        dx := dx + sz
      end
    end
```

```
        end ;
        if sy <> rparent
        then begin
            if sy = semicolon
            then insymbol
            else begin
                error(14);
                if sy = comma then insymbol
            end ;
            test([ident,varsy], [rparent]+fsys, 6)
        end
    end  { while } ;

    if sy = rparent
    then begin
        insymbol;
        test([semicolon,colon], fsys, 6)
    end else error(4)
end  { parameterlist } ;

procedure constdec;

var     c: conrec;
begin
    insymbol;
    test([ident], blockbegsys, 2);
    while sy = ident do
    begin
        enter(id,konstant); insymbol;
        if sy = eql
        then insymbol
        else begin
            error(16);
            if sy = becomes then insymbol
        end ;
        constant([semicolon,comma,ident]+fsys,c);
        tab[t].typ := c.tp;
        tab[t].ref := 0;
        if c.tp = reals
        then begin
            enterreal(c.r); tab[t].adr := cl
        end else tab[t].adr := c.i;
        testsemicolon
    end
end  { constdec } ;

procedure typedeclaration;

var     tp: types;
        rf, sz, tl: integer;
begin
    insymbol;
    test([ident], blockbegsys, 2);
    while sy = ident do
    begin
        enter(id,type1);
        tl := t; insymbol;
        if sy = eql
        then insymbol
        else begin
            error(16);
            if sy = becomes then insymbol
        end ;
        typ([semicolon,comma,ident]+fsys, tp, rf, sz);
        with tab[tl] do
        begin
            typ := tp; ref := rf; adr :=sz
        end;
        testsemicolon
    end
end  { typedeclaration } ;
```

```
procedure variabledeclaration;

var    tp: types;
       t0, t1, rf, sz: integer;
begin
  insymbol;
  while sy = ident do
  begin
    t0 := t; entervariable;
    while sy = comma do
    begin
      insymbol; entervariable;
    end ;
    if sy = colon then insymbol else error(5);
    t1 := t;
    typ([semicolon,comma,ident]+fsys, tp, rf, sz);
    while t0 < t1 do
    begin
      t0 := t0+1;
      with tab[t0] do
      begin
        typ := tp;    ref := rf;
        lev := level; adr := dx;
        normal := true;
        dx := dx + sz
      end
    end ;
    testsemicolon
  end
end { variabledeclaration } ;

procedure procdeclaration;

var    isfun: boolean;
begin
  isfun := sy = funcsy;
  insymbol;
  if sy <> ident
  then begin
    error(2); id := '
  end ;
  if isfun then enter(id,funktion) else enter(id,prozedure);
  tab[t].normal := true;
  insymbol;
  block([semicolon]+fsys, isfun, level+1);
  if sy = semicolon then insymbol else error(14);
  emit(32+ord(isfun))       { exit }
end { procceduredeclaration } ;


procedure statement(fsys: symset);

var    i: integer;
       x: item;

  procedure expression(fsys: symset; var x: item); forward;

  procedure selector(fsys: symset; var v:item);

  var    x: item;
         a,j: integer;
  begin { sy in [lparent, lbrack, period] }
    repeat
      if sy = period
      then begin
        insymbol;    { field selector }
        if sy <> ident
        then error(2)
        else begin
          if v.typ <> records
          then error(31)
```

```
        else begin   { search field identifier }
          j := btab[v.ref] .last;
          tab[0].name := id;
          while tab[j].name <> id do j := tab[j].link;
          if j = 0 then error(0);
          v.typ := tab[j].typ;
          v.ref := tab[j].ref;
          a := tab[j].adr;
          if a <> 0 then emitl(9,a)
        end ;
        insymbol
      end
    end else begin   { array selector }
      if sy <> lbrack then error(11);
      repeat
        insymbol;
        expression(fsys+[comma,rbrack], x);
        if v.typ <> arrays
        then error(28)
        else begin
          a := v.ref;
          if atab[a].inxtyp <> x.typ
          then error(26)
          else if atab[a].elsize = 1
              then emitl(20,a)
              else emitl(21,a);
          v.typ := atab[a].eltyp;
          v.ref := atab[a].elref
        end
      until sy <> comma;

      if sy = rbrack
      then insymbol
      else begin
        error(12);
        if sy = rparent then insymbol
      end
    end
  until not (sy in [lbrack,lparent,period]);

  test(fsys, [], 6)
end   { selector } ;

procedure call(fsys: symset; i: integer);

var    x: item;
       lastp, cp, k: integer;

begin
  emitl(18,i);   { mark stack }
  lastp := btab[tab[i].ref].lastpar;
  cp := i;
  if sy = lparent
  then begin   { actual parameter list }
    repeat
      insymbol;
      if cp >= lastp
      then error(39)
      else begin
        cp := cp+1;
        if tab[cp].normal
        then begin   { value parameter }
          expression(fsys+[comma,colon,rparent], x);
          if x.typ=tab[cp].typ
          then begin
            if x.ref <> tab[cp].ref
            then error(36)
            else if x.typ = arrays
                then emitl(22,atab[x.ref].size)
                else if x.typ = records
                    then emitl(22,btab[x.ref].vsize)
```

```
                 end else if (x.typ=ints) and (tab[cp].typ=reals)
                          then emit1(26,0)
                          else if x.typ<>notyp then error(36);
              end else begin  { variable parameter }
                 if sy <> ident
                 then error(2)
                 else begin
                    k := loc(id);
                    insymbol;
                    if k <> 0
                    then begin
                       if tab[k].obj <> vvariable then error(37);
                       x.typ := tab[k].typ;
                       x.ref := tab[k].ref;
                       if tab[k].normal
                       then emit2(0,tab[k].lev,tab[k].adr)
                       else emit2(1,tab[k].lev,tab[k].adr);
                       if sy in [lbrack,lparent,period]
                       then selector(fsys+[comma,colon,rparent], x);
                       if (x.typ<>tab[cp].typ) or (x.ref<>tab[cp].ref)
                       then error(36)
                    end
                 end
              end {variable parameter}
           end ;
           test([comma,rparent], fsys, 6)
        until sy <> comma;

     if sy = rparent then insymbol else error(4)
     end ;

     if cp < lastp then error(39); { too few actual parameters }
     emit1(19, btab[tab[i].ref].psize-1);
     if tab[i].lev < level then emit2(3, tab[i].lev, level)
  end  { call } ;

function resulttype(a,b: types): types;

begin
  if (a>reals) or (b>reals)
  then begin
     error(33);
     resulttype := notyp;
  end else if (a=notyp) or (b=notyp)
           then resulttype := notyp
           else if a=ints
                   then if b=ints
                           then resulttype := ints
                           else begin
                              resulttype := reals; emit1(26,1)
                           end
                   else begin
                      resulttype := reals;
                      if b=ints then emit1(26,0)
                   end
end  { resulttype } ;

  procedure expression {fsys:symset; var x:item};

  var    y :item;
         op:symbol;

    procedure simpleexpression(fsys:symset; var x:item);

    var    y :item;
           op:symbol;

      procedure term(fsys:symset; var x:item);

      var    y :item;
             op:symbol;
             ts:typset;
```

```
          procedure factor(fsys:symset; var x:item);

          var     i,f: integer;

            procedure standfct(n: integer);

            var     ts: typset;

            begin { standard function no. n }
              if sy = lparent
              then insymbol
              else error(9);
              if n < 17
              then begin
                expression(fsys+[rparent],x);

              case n of
{ abs,sqr }       0,2: begin
                         ts := [ints,reals];
                         tab[i].typ := x.typ;
                         if x.typ = reals then n := n+1
                       end ;

{ odd,chr }       4,5: ts := [ints];

{ ord }             6: ts := [ints,bools,chars];

{ succ,pred }     7,8: begin
                         ts := [ints,bools,chars];
                         tab[i].typ := x.typ
                       end ;

{ round,trunc } 9,10,11,12,13,14,15,16:
{ sin,cos,... }     begin
                         ts := [ints,reals];
                         if x.typ = ints then emit1(26,0)
                       end ;
                  end ; { case }

              if x.typ in ts
              then emit1(8,n)
              else if x.typ <> notyp
                   then error(48);
              end else begin      { n in [17,18] }
                if sy <> ident
                then error(2)
                else if id <> 'input
                     then error(0)
                     else insymbol;
                emit1(8,n);
              end ;
              x.typ := tab[i].typ;
              if sy = rparent then insymbol else error(4)
            end { standfct } ;

          begin { factor }
            x.typ := notyp;
            x.ref := 0;
            test(facbegsys, fsys, 58);
            while sy in facbegsys do
            begin
              if sy = ident
              then begin
                i := loc(id);
                insymbol;
                with tab[i] do

                  case obj of
```

```
konstant: begin
            x.typ := typ;
            x.ref := 0;
            if x.typ = reals
            then emit1(25,adr)
            else emit1(24,adr)
          end ;

vvariable: begin
            x.typ := typ;
            x.ref := ref;
            if sy in [lbrack,lparent,period]
            then begin
              if normal then f := 0 else f := 1;
              emit2(f, lev, adr);
              selector(fsys,x);
              if x.typ in stantyps then emit(34)
            end else begin
              if x.typ in stantyps
              then if normal
                      then f := 1
                      else f := 2
              else if normal then f := 0 else f := 1;
              emit2(f, lev, adr)
            end
          end ;

typel, prozedure: error(44);

funktion : begin
            x.typ := typ;
            if lev <> 0
            then call(fsys, i)
            else standfct(adr)
          end

        end { case,with }

        end else if sy in [charcon,intcon,realcon]
                then begin
                  if sy = realcon
                  then begin
                    x.typ := reals;
                    enterreal(rnum);
                    emit1(25, cl)
                  end else begin
                    if sy = charcon
                    then x.typ := chars
                    else x.typ := ints;
                    emit1(24, inum)
                  end ;
                  x.ref := 0;
                  insymbol
                end else if sy = lparent
                        then begin
                          insymbol;
                          expression(fsys+[rparent], x);
                          if sy = rparent
                          then insymbol
                          else error(4)
                        end else if sy = notsy
                                then begin
                                  insymbol;
                                  factor(fsys,x);
                                  if x.typ=bools
                                  then emit(35)
                                  else if x.typ<>notyp
                                          then error(32)
                                end ;
        test(fsys, facbegsys, 6)
      end { while }
    end { factor } ;
```

```
begin { term }
  factor(fsys+[times,rdiv,idiv,imod,andsy], x);
  while sy in [times,rdiv,idiv,imod,andsy] do
  begin
    op := sy;
    insymbol;
    factor(fsys+[times,rdiv,idiv,imod,andsy], y);
    if op = times
    then begin
      x.typ := resulttype(x.typ, y.typ);

      case x.typ of
notyp: ;
ints : emit(57);
reals: emit(60);
      end

    end else if op = rdiv
         then begin
           if x.typ = ints
           then begin
             emit1(26,1);
             x.typ := reals
           end ;
           if y.typ = ints
           then begin
             emit1(26,0);
             y.typ := reals
           end ;
           if (x.typ=reals) and (y.typ=reals)
           then emit(61)
           else begin
             if (x.typ<>notyp) and (y.typ<>notyp)
             then error(33);
             x.typ := notyp
           end
         end else if op = andsy
              then begin
                if (x.typ=bools) and (y.typ=bools)
                then emit(56)
                else begin
                  if (x.typ<>notyp) and (y.typ<>notyp)
                  then error(32);
                  x.typ := notyp
                end
              end else begin      { op in [idiv,imod] }
                if (x.typ=ints) and (y.typ=ints)
                then if op=idiv
                     then emit(58)
                     else emit(59)
                else begin
                  if (x.typ<>notyp) and (y.typ<>notyp)
                  then error(34);
                  x.typ := notyp
                end
              end
  end {while}
end { term } ;

begin { simpleexpression }
  if sy in [plus,minus]
  then begin
    op := sy;
    insymbol;
    term(fsys+[plus,minus], x);
    if x.typ > reals
    then error(33)
    else if op = minus
         then emit(36)
  end else term(fsys+[plus,minus,orsy], x);
```

```
      while sy in [plus,minus,orsy] do
      begin
        op := sy;
        insymbol;
        term(fsys+[plus,minus,orsy], y);
        if op = orsy
        then begin
          if (x.typ=bools) and (y.typ=bools)
          then emit(51)
          else begin
            if (x.typ<>notyp) and (y.typ<>notyp)
            then error(32);
            x.typ := notyp
          end
        end else begin
          x.typ := resulttype(x.typ, y.typ);

          case x.typ of
    notyp: ;
    ints : if op = plus
           then emit(52)
           else emit(53);
    reals: if op = plus
           then emit(54)
           else emit(55)
           end {case}

        end
      end {while}
    end { simpleexpression } ;

begin { expression }
  simpleexpression(fsys+[eql,neq,lss,leq,gtr,geq], x);
  if sy in [eql,neq,lss,leq,gtr,geq]
  then begin
    op := sy;
    insymbol;
    simpleexpression(fsys, y);
    if (x.typ in [notyp,ints,bools,chars]) and (x.typ = y.typ)
    then case op of

        eql: emit(45);
        neq: emit(46);
        lss: emit(47);
        leq: emit(48);
        gtr: emit(49);
        geq: emit(50);

        end
        else begin
          if x.typ = ints
          then begin
            x.typ := reals;
            emit1(26,1)
          end else if y.typ = ints
                    then begin
                      y.typ := reals;
                      emit1(26,0)
                    end ;
          if (x.typ=reals) and (y.typ=reals)
          then case op of

              eql: emit(39);
              neq: emit(40);
              lss: emit(41);
              leq: emit(42);
              gtr: emit(43);
              geq: emit(44);

              end
```

```
                  else error(35)
            end ;
            x.typ := bools
      end
end { expression } ;

procedure assignment(lv,ad: integer);

var     x,y: item;
        f  : integer;
begin                       { tab[i].obj in [variable,prozedure] }
   x.typ := tab[i].typ;
   x.ref := tab[i].ref;
   if tab[i].normal then f := 0 else f := 1;
   emit2(f, lv, ad);
   if sy in [lbrack,lparent,period]
   then selector([becomes,eql]+fsys, x);

   if sy = becomes
   then insymbol
   else begin
      error(51);
      if sy = eql then insymbol
   end ;

   expression(fsys, y);
   if x.typ = y.typ
   then if x.typ in stantyps
        then emit(38)
        else if x.ref <> y.ref
             then error(46)
             else if x.typ = arrays
                  then emit1(23, atab[x.ref].size)
                  else emit1(23, btab[x.ref].vsize)
   else if (x.typ=reals) and (y.typ=ints)
   then begin
      emit1(26,0);
      emit(38)
   end else if (x.typ<>notyp) and (y.typ<>notyp)
             then error(46)
end { assignment } ;

procedure compoundstatement;

begin
   insymbol;
   statement([semicolon,endsy]+fsys);
   while sy in [semicolon]+statbegsys do
   begin
      if sy = semicolon
      then insymbol
      else error(14);
      statement([semicolon,endsy]+fsys)
   end ;
   if sy = endsy then insymbol else error(57)
end { compoundstatemenet } ;

procedure ifstatement;

var     x: item;
        lc1,lc2: integer;
begin
   insymbol;
   expression(fsys+[thensy,dosy], x);
   if not (x.typ in [bools,notyp])
   then error(17);
   lc1 := lc;
   emit(11);        { jmpc }

   if sy = thensy
   then insymbol
```

```
    else begin
        error(52);
        if sy = dosy
        then insymbol
    end ;

    statement(fsys+[elsesy]);

    if sy = elsesy
    then begin
        insymbol;                      lc2 := lc;
        emit(10);            code[lc1].y := lc;
        statement(fsys); code[lc2].y := lc
    end
    else code[lc1].y := lc
end { ifstatement } ;

procedure casestatement;

var     x: item;
        i,j,k,lc1: integer;
        casetab: array [1..csmax] of
                    packed record
                        val, lc: index
                    end ;
        exittab: array [1..csmax] of integer;

    procedure caselabel;

    var     lab: conrec;
            k  : integer;
    begin
        constant(fsys+[comma,colon], lab);
        if lab.tp <> x.typ
        then error(47)
        else if i = csmax
            then fatal(6)
            else begin
                i := i+1;        k := 0;
                casetab[i].val := lab.i;
                casetab[i].lc   := lc;
                repeat
                    k := k+1
                until casetab[k].val = lab.i;

                if k < i then error(1);    { multiple definition }
            end
    end { caselabel } ;

    procedure onecase;

    begin
        if sy in constbegsys
        then begin
            caselabel;
            while sy = comma do
            begin
                insymbol; caselabel
            end ;
            if sy = colon
            then insymbol else error(5);
            statement([semicolon,endsy]+fsys);
            j := j+1;
            exittab[j] := lc; emit(10)
        end
    end { onecase } ;

begin {casestatement}
    insymbol;
    i := 0;     j := 0;
    expression(fsys+[ofsy,comma,colon], x);
```

```
      if not (x.typ in [ints,bools,chars,notyp])
      then error(23);
      lcl := lc; emit(12);  { jmpx }

      if sy = ofsy then insymbol else error(8);
      onecase;
      while sy = semicolon do
      begin
         insymbol;
         onecase
      end ;
      code[lcl].y := lc;
      for k := 1 to i do
      begin
         emit1(13,casetab[k].val);
         emit1(13,casetab[k].lc)
      end ;
      emit1(10,0);
      for k := 1 to j do code[exittab[k]].y := lc;
      if sy = endsy then insymbol else error(57)
   end { casestatement } ;

   procedure repeatstatement;

   var     x  : item;
           lcl: integer;
   begin
      lcl := lc;
      insymbol;
      statement([semicolon,untilsy]+fsys);
      while sy in [semicolon]+statbegsys do
      begin
         if sy = semicolon then insymbol else error(14);
         statement([semicolon,untilsy]+fsys)
      end ;
      if sy = untilsy
      then begin
         insymbol;
         expression(fsys, x);
         if not (x.typ in [bools,notyp]) then error(17);
         emit1(11,lcl)
      end else error(53)
   end { repeatstatement } ;

   procedure whilestatement;

   var     x: item;
           lcl,lc2: integer;
   begin
      insymbol;
      lcl := lc;
      expression(fsys+[dosy], x);
      if not (x.typ in [bools,notyp]) then error(17);
      lc2 := lc; emit(11);

      if sy = dosy then insymbol else error(54);
      statement(fsys);
      emit1(10,lcl);
      code[lc2].y := lc
   end { whilestatement } ;

   procedure forstatement;

   var     cvt: types;
           x  : item;
           i,f,lcl,lc2: integer;
   begin
      insymbol;
      if sy = ident
```

```
          then begin
            i := loc(id);
            insymbol;
            if i = 0
            then cvt := ints
            else if tab[i].obj = vvariable
                 then begin
                   cvt := tab[i].typ;
                   if not tab[i].normal
                   then error(37)
                   else emit2(0, tab[i].lev, tab[i].adr);
                   if not (cvt in [notyp,ints,bools,chars]) then error(18)
                 end else begin
                   error(37); cvt := ints
                 end
        end else skip([becomes,tosy,downtosy,dosy]+fsys, 2);

        if sy = becomes
        then begin
          insymbol;
          expression([tosy,downtosy,dosy]+fsys, x);
          if x.typ <> cvt then error(19);
        end else skip([tosy,downtosy,dosy]+fsys, 51);
        f := 14;

        if sy in [tosy, downtosy]
        then begin
          if sy = downtosy then f := 16;
          insymbol;
          expression([dosy]+fsys, x);
          if x.typ <> cvt then error(19)
        end else skip([dosy]+fsys, 55);

        lc1 := lc; emit(f);
        if sy = dosy then insymbol else error(54);
        lc2 := lc;
        statement(fsys);
        emit1(f+1,lc2);
        code[lc1].y := lc
      end { forstatement } ;

    procedure standproc(n: integer);

    var    i,f: integer;
           x,y: item;
    begin

      case n of

1,2:  begin { read }
        if not iflag
        then begin
          error(20); iflag := true
        end ;
        if sy = lparent
        then begin
          repeat
            insymbol;
            if sy <> ident
            then error(2)
            else begin
              i := loc(id);
              insymbol;
              if i <> 0
              then if tab[i].obj <> vvariable
                   then error(37)
                   else begin
                     x.typ := tab[i].typ;
                     x.ref := tab[i].ref;
                     if tab[i].normal then f := 0 else f := 1;
                     emit2(f, tab[i].lev, tab[i].adr);
```

```
                    if sy in [lbrack,lparent,period]
                    then selector(fsys+[comma,rparent], x);
                    if x.typ in [ints,reals,chars,notyp]
                    then emit1(27,ord(x.typ))
                    else error(41)
                  end
          end ;
          test([comma,rparent], fsys, 6);
        until sy <> comma;

        if sy = rparent then insymbol else error(4)
      end ;
      if n = 2 then emit(62)
    end ;

3,4: begin { write }
       if sy = lparent
       then begin

         repeat
           insymbol;
           if sy = stringcon
           then begin
             emit1(24,sleng);
             emit1(28,inum);
             insymbol
           end else begin
             expression(fsys+[comma,colon,rparent], x);
             if not (x.typ in stantyps) then error(41);
             if sy = colon
             then begin
               insymbol;
               expression(fsys+[comma,colon,rparent], y);
               if y.typ <> ints then error(43);
               if sy = colon
               then begin
                 if x.typ <> reals then error(42);
                 insymbol;
                 expression(fsys+[comma,rparent], y);
                 if y.typ <> ints then error(43);
                 emit(37)
               end else emit1(30, ord(x.typ))
             end else emit1(29, ord(x.typ))
           end
         until sy <> comma;

         if sy = rparent then insymbol else error(4)
       end ;
       if n = 4 then emit(63)
     end ; {write}

   end { case }

 end { standproc } ;

begin { statement }
  if sy in statbegsys+[ident]
  then case sy of

    ident: begin
             i := loc(id);
             insymbol;
             if i <> 0
             then case tab[i].obj of

      konstant, typel: error(45);
           vvariable: assignment(tab[i].lev, tab[i].adr);
           prozedure: if tab[i].lev <> 0
                      then call(fsys, i)
                      else standproc(tab[i].adr);
```

```
                    funktion: if tab[i].ref = display[level]
                              then assignment(tab[i].lev+1, 0)
                              else error(45)
                          end{case}

               end ;

  beginsy: compoundstatement;
     ifsy: ifstatement;
   casesy: casestatement;
  whilesy: whilestatement;
 repeatsy: repeatstatement;
    forsy: forstatement;

       end; {case}

 test(fsys, [], 14)
 end { statement } ;

begin { block }
 dx := 5; prt := t;
 if level > lmax then fatal(5);
 test([lparent,colon,semicolon], fsys, 14);

 enterblock;
          prb := b;        display[level] := b;
 tab[prt].typ := notyp;    tab[prt].ref := prb;
 if (sy = lparent) and (level > 1) then parameterlist;
 btab[prb].lastpar := t;btab[prb].psize := dx;

 if isfun
 then if sy = colon
      then begin
        insymbol;    { function type }
        if sy = ident
        then begin
          x := loc(id);
          insymbol;
          if x <> 0
          then if tab[x].obj <> typel
               then error(29)
               else if tab[x].typ in stantyps
                    then tab[prt].typ := tab[x].typ
                    else error(15)
        end else skip([semicolon]+fsys, 2)
      end else error(5);
 if sy = semicolon then insymbol else error(14);

 repeat
    if sy = constsy then constdec;
    if sy = typesy then typedeclaration;
    if sy = varsy then variabledeclaration;
    btab[prb].vsize := dx;
    while sy in [procsy,funcsy] do procdeclaration;
    test([beginsy], blockbegsys+statbegsys, 56)
 until sy in statbegsys;

 tab[prt].adr := lc;
 insymbol;
 statement([semicolon,endsy]+fsys);

 while sy in [semicolon]+statbegsys do
 begin
    if sy = semicolon then insymbol else error(14);
    statement([semicolon,endsy]+fsys)
 end ;
 if sy = endsy then insymbol else error(57);
 test(fsys+[period], [], 6)
 end { block } ;

    procedure interpret;
```

```
var     ir: order;         { instruction buffer }
        pc: integer;       { program counter }
         t: integer;       { top stack index }
         b: integer;       { base index }
        h1,h2,h3,h4: integer;
        lncnt, ocnt, blkcnt, chrcnt: integer;      { counters }

        ps: (run,fin,caschk,divchk,inxchk,stkchk,linchk,lngchk,redchk);

        fld     : array [1..4] of integer;      { default field widths }
        display: array [0..lmax] of integer;
        s       : array [1..stacksize] of      { blockmark:              }
            record
              case cn:types of                  {    s[b+0] = fct result  }
              ints:   (i: integer);             {    s[b+1] = return adr  }
              reals:  (r: real);                {    s[b+2] = static link }
              bools:  (b: boolean);             {    s[b+3] = dynamic link }
              chars:  (c: char)                 {    s[b+4] = table index  }
            end ;

procedure dump;

var     p,h3 :integer;

begin
  h3:=tab[h2].lev;
  writeln(psout);writeln(psout);
  writeln(psout,'          calling ',tab[h2].name);
  writeln(psout,'            level ',h3:4);
  writeln(psout,' start of  code ',pc:4);
  writeln(psout);writeln(psout);
  writeln(psout,' contents of display '); writeln(psout);

  for p:=h3  downto 0 do writeln(psout,p:4,display[p]:6);

  writeln(psout);writeln(psout);
  writeln(psout,' top of stack    ',t:4,' frame base ':14,b:4);
  writeln(psout);writeln(psout);
  writeln(psout,'stack contents':20); writeln(psout);

  for p:=t  downto 1 do writeln(psout,p:14,s[p].i:8);

  writeln(psout,'< = = = >':22)
end; { dump }

procedure inter0;
begin
  case ir.f of

  0: begin { load address }
       t := t+1;
       if t > stacksize
       then ps := stkchk
       else s[t].i := display[ir.x] + ir.y
     end ;

  1: begin { load value }
       t := t+1;
       if t > stacksize
       then ps := stkchk
       else s[t] := s[display[ir.x] + ir.y]
     end ;

  2: begin { load indirect }
       t := t+1;
       if t > stacksize
       then ps := stkchk
       else s[t] := s[s[display[ir.x] + ir.y].i]
     end ;
```

```
3: begin { update display }
     h1 := ir.y; h2 := ir.x; h3 := b;
     repeat
       display[h1] := h3; h1 := h1-1; h3 := s[h3+2].i
     until h1 = h2
   end ;

8: case ir.y of
     0:  s[t].i := abs(s[t].i);
     1:  s[t].r := abs(s[t].r);
     2:  s[t].i := sqr(s[t].i);
     3:  s[t].r := sqr(s[t].r);
     4:  s[t].b := odd(s[t].i);
     5:  s[t].c := chr(s[t].i);
     6:  s[t].i := ord(s[t].c);
     7:  s[t].c := succ(s[t].c);
     8:  s[t].c := pred(s[t].c);
     9:  s[t].i := round(s[t].r);
     10: s[t].i := trunc(s[t].r);
     11: s[t].r := sin(s[t].r);
     12: s[t].r := cos(s[t].r);
     13: s[t].r := exp(s[t].r);
     14: s[t].r := ln(s[t].r);
     15: s[t].r := sqrt(s[t].r);
     16: s[t].r := atan(s[t].r);
     17: begin t := t+1;
           if t > stacksize
           then ps := stkchk else s[t].b := eof(prd)
         end ;
     18: begin
           t := t+1;
           if t > stacksize
           then ps := stkchk else s[t].b := eoln(prd)
         end ;
   end ;

  9: s[t].i := s[t].i + ir.y;    { offset }
  end { case ir.y }
end; { inter0 }

procedure inter1;

begin
  case ir.f of

  10: pc := ir.y; { jump }
  11: begin { conditional jump }
        if not s[t].b then pc := ir.y;
        t := t-1
      end ;

  12: begin { switch }
        h1 := s[t].i;        t := t-1;
        h2 := ir.y;          h3 := 0;
        repeat
          if code[h2].f <> 13
          then begin
            h3 := 1;
            ps := caschk
          end else if code[h2].y = h1
                  then begin
                    h3 := 1;
                    pc := code[h2+1].y
                  end else h2 := h2 + 2
        until h3 <> 0
      end ;
```

```
14: begin { forlup }
      h1 := s[t-1].i;
      if h1 <= s[t].i
      then s[s[t-2].i].i := h1
      else begin
        t := t-3;
        pc := ir.y
      end
    end ;

15: begin { for2up }
      h2 := s[t-2].i;
      h1 := s[h2].i + 1;
      if h1 <= s[t].i
      then begin
        s[h2].i := h1; pc := ir.y
      end else t := t-3;
    end ;

16: begin { forldown }
      h1 := s[t-1].i;
      if h1 >= s[t].i
      then s[s[t-2].i].i := h1
      else begin
        pc := ir.y; t := t-3
      end
    end ;

17: begin { for2down }
      h2 := s[t-2].i;
      h1 := s[h2].i - 1;
      if h1 >= s[t].i
      then begin
        s[h2].i := h1; pc := ir.y
      end else t := t-3;
    end ;

18: begin { mark stack }
      h1 := btab[tab[ir.y].ref].vsize;
      if t+h1 > stacksize
      then ps := stkchk
      else begin
        t := t+5;
        s[t-1].i := h1-1;    s[t].i := ir.y
      end
    end ;

19: begin { call }
      h1 := t - ir.y;                { h1 points to base }
      h2 := s[h1+4].i;               { h2 points to tab }
      h3 := tab[h2].lev;   display[h3+1] := h1;
      h4 := s[h1+3].i + h1;
      s[h1+1].i := pc;     s[h1+2].i := display[h3];
      s[h1+3].i := b;
      for h3 := t+1 to h4 do s[h3].i := 0;
      b := h1;      t := h4;
      pc := tab[h2].adr;
      if stackdump then dump
    end ;
  end { case }

end; { inter1 }

procedure inter2;

begin
  case ir.f of

20: begin { index1 }
      h1 := ir.y;        { h1 points to atab }
      h2 := atab[h1].low;
      h3 := s[t].i;
```

```
          if h3 < h2
          then ps := inxchk
          else if h3 > atab[h1].high
                  then ps := inxchk
                  else begin
                       t := t-1;
                       s[t].i := s[t].i + (h3-h2)
                       end
     end ;

21: begin { index }
     h1 := ir.y;         { h1 points to atab }
     h2 := atab[h1].low;
     h3 := s[t].i;
     if h3 < h2
     then ps := inxchk
     else if h3 > atab[h1].high
             then ps := inxchk
             else begin
                  t := t-1;
                  s[t].i := s[t].i + (h3-h2)*atab[h1].elsize
                  end
     end ;

22: begin { load block }
     h1 := s[t].i;      t := t-1;
     h2 := ir.y + t;
     if h2 > stacksize
     then ps := stkchk
     else while t < h2 do
             begin
             t := t+1;
             s[t] := s[h1];     h1 := h1+1
             end
     end ;

23: begin { copy block }
     h1 := s[t-1].i;
     h2 := s[t].i;
     h3 := h1 + ir.y;
     while h1 < h3 do
     begin
          s[h1] := s[h2];
          h1 := h1+1;     h2 := h2+1
     end ;
     t := t-2
     end ;

24: begin { literal }
     t := t+1;
     if t > stacksize
     then ps := stkchk else s[t].i := ir.y
     end ;

25: begin { load real }
     t := t+1;
     if t > stacksize
     then ps := stkchk else s[t].r := rconst[ir.y]
     end ;

26: begin { float }
     h1 := t - ir.y;
     s[h1].r := s[h1].i
     end ;

27: begin { read }
     if eot(prd)
     then ps := redchk
```

```
        else case ir.y of
             1: read(prd,s[s[t].i].i);
             2: read(prd,s[s[t].i].r);
             4: read(prd,s[s[t].i].c);
               end ;

        t := t-1
      end ;

  28: begin { write string }
         h1 := s[t].i;
         h2 := ir.y;     t := t-1;
         chrcnt := chrcnt+h1;
         if chrcnt > lineleng then ps := lngchk;
         repeat
             write(prr,stab[h2]);
             h1 := h1-1;
             h2 := h2+1
         until h1 = 0
      end ;


  29: begin { writel }
         chrcnt := chrcnt + fld[ir.y];
         if chrcnt > lineleng
         then ps := lngchk
         else case ir.y of
             1: write(prr,s[t].i: fld[1]);
             2: write(prr,s[t].r: fld[2]);
             3: if s[t].b then write ('true') else write ('false');
             4: write(prr,chr(s[t].i));
               end ;

        t := t-1
      end ;
   end { case }
end; { inter2 }

procedure inter3;

begin
  case ir.f of

  30: begin { write2 }
         chrcnt := chrcnt + s[t].i;
         if chrcnt > lineleng
         then ps := lngchk
         else case ir.y of
             1: write(prr,s[t-1].i: s[t].i);
             2: write(prr,s[t-1].r: s[t].i);
             3: if s[t-1].b then write ('true') else write ('false');
             4: write(prr,chr(s[t-1].i): s[t].i);
               end ;

        t := t-2
      end ;

  31: ps := fin;

  32: begin { exit procedure }
        t := b-1;
        pc := s[b+1].i;     b := s[b+3].i
      end ;

  33: begin { exit function }
        t := b;
        pc := s[b+1].i;     b := s[b+3].i
      end ;

  34: s[t] := s[s[t].i];

  35: s[t].b := not s[t].b;
```

```
36: s[t].i := - s[t].i;

37: begin
        chrcnt := chrcnt + s[t-1].i;
        if chrcnt > lineleng
        then ps := lngchk
        else write(prr,s[t-2].r: s[t-1].i);
        t := t-3
    end ;

38: begin { store }
        s[s[t-1].i] := s[t];
        t := t-2
    end ;

39: begin
        t := t-1;
        s[t].b := s[t].r = s[t+1].r
    end ;
  end { case }
end; { inter3 }

procedure inter4;

begin
  case ir.f of

40: begin
        t := t-1;
        s[t].b := s[t].r <> s[t+1].r
    end ;

41: begin
        t := t-1;
        s[t].b := s[t].r < s[t+1].r
    end ;

42: begin
        t := t-1;
        s[t].b := s[t].r <= s[t+1].r
    end ;

43: begin
        t := t-1;
        s[t].b := s[t].r > s[t+1].r
    end ;

44: begin
        t := t-1;
        s[t].b := s[t].r >= s[t+1].r
    end ;

45: begin
        t := t-1;
        s[t].b := s[t].i = s[t+1].i
    end ;

46: begin
        t := t-1;
        s[t].b := s[t].i <> s[t+1].i
    end ;

47: begin
        t := t-1;
        s[t].b := s[t].i < s[t+1].i
    end ;

48: begin
        t := t-1;
        s[t].b := s[t].i <= s[t+1].i
    end ;
```

```
49: begin
        t := t-1;
        s[t].b := s[t].i > s[t+1].i
      end ;

  end { case }
end; { inter4 }

procedure inter5;

begin
  case ir.f of

  50: begin
        t := t-1;
        s[t].b := s[t].i >= s[t+1].i
      end ;

  51: begin
        t := t-1;
        s[t].b := s[t].b or s[t+1].b
      end ;

  52: begin
        t := t-1;
        s[t].i := s[t].i + s[t+1].i
      end ;

  53: begin
        t := t-1;
        s[t].i := s[t].i - s[t+1].i
      end ;

  54: begin
        t := t-1;
        s[t].r := s[t].r + s[t+1].r;
      end ;

  55: begin
        t := t-1;
        s[t].r := s[t].r - s[t+1].r;
      end ;

  56: begin
        t := t-1;
        s[t].b := s[t].b and s[t+1].b
      end ;

  57: begin
        t := t-1;
        s[t].i := s[t].i * s[t+1].i
      end ;

  58: begin
        t := t-1;
        if s[t+1].i = 0
        then ps := divchk
        else s[t].i := s[t].i div s[t+1].i
      end ;

  59: begin
        t := t-1;
        if s[t+1].i = 0
        then ps := divchk
        else s[t].i := s[t].i mod s[t+1].i
      end ;

  end { case }
end; { inter5 }

procedure inter6;
```

```
begin
   case ir.f of

  60: begin
        t := t-1;
        s[t].r := s[t].r * s[t+1].r;
      end ;

  61: begin
        t := t-1;
        s[t].r := s[t].r / s[t+1].r;
      end ;

  62: if eof(prd) then ps := redchk else readln;

  63: begin
        writeln(prr);
        lncnt := lncnt + 1;    chrcnt := 0;
        if lncnt > linelimit then ps := linchk
      end

    end { case } ;
end; { inter6 }

begin { interpret }
      s[1].i := 0;      s[2].i := 0;
      s[3].i := -1;     s[4].i := btab[1].last;
   display[1] := 0;        t := btab[2].vsize - 1;
         b := 0;          pc := tab[s[4].i].adr;
      lncnt := 0;       ocnt := 0;
      chrcnt := 0;        ps := run;

      fld[1] := 10;     fld[2] := 22;
      fld[3] := 10;     fld[4] := 1;

   repeat
      ir := code[pc];
      pc := pc+1;       ocnt := ocnt + 1;

      case ir.f div 10 of
         0: inter0;
         1: inter1;
         2: inter2;
         3: inter3;
         4: inter4;
         5: inter5;
         6: inter6;
      end; { case }
   until ps <> run;

   if ps <> fin
   then begin
      writeln(prr);
      write(prr,' halt at', pc:5, ' because of ');
      case ps of
         caschk: writeln(prr,'undefined case');
         divchk: writeln(prr,'division by 0');
         inxchk: writeln(prr,'invalid index');
         stkchk: writeln(prr,'storage overflow');
         linchk: writeln(prr,'too much output');
         lngchk: writeln(prr,'line too long');
         redchk: writeln(prr,'reading past end of file');
      end ;

   h1 := b; blkcnt := 10;    { post mortem dump }
   repeat
      writeln(prr); blkcnt := blkcnt - 1;
      if blkcnt = 0 then h1 := 0; h2 := s[h1+4].i;
      if h1<>0
      then writeln(prr,'  ', tab[h2].name, ' called at', s[h1+1].i: 5);
      h2 := btab[tab[h2].ref].last;
```

```
       while h2 <> 0 do
          with tab[h2] do
          begin
             if obj = vvariable
             then if typ in stantyps
                  then begin
                     write(prr,'        ', name, ' = ');
                     if normal then h3 := h1+adr else h3 := s[h1+adr].i;
                     case typ of
                        ints : writeln(prr,s[h3].i);
                        reals: writeln(prr,s[h3].r);
                        bools: if s[h3].b
                               then writeln(prr,'true')
                               else writeln(prr,'false');
                        chars: writeln(prr,chr(s[h3].i mod 64))
                     end
                  end ;
             h2 := link
          end ;
          h1 := s[h1+3].i
       until h1 < 0;
    end ;

    writeln(prr); writeln(prr,ocnt, ' steps');

 end ; { interpret }

 procedure setup;

 begin
    key[ 1] := 'and       '; key[ 2] := 'array     ';
    key[ 3] := 'begin     '; key[ 4] := 'case      ';
    key[ 5] := 'const     '; key[ 6] := 'div       ';
    key[ 7] := 'do        '; key[ 8] := 'downto    ';
    key[ 9] := 'else      '; key[10] := 'end       ';
    key[11] := 'for       '; key[12] := 'function  ';
    key[13] := 'if        '; key[14] := 'mod       ';
    key[15] := 'not       '; key[16] := 'of        ';
    key[17] := 'or        '; key[18] := 'procedure ';
    key[19] := 'program   '; key[20] := 'record    ';
    key[21] := 'repeat    '; key[22] := 'then      ';
    key[23] := 'to        '; key[24] := 'type      ';
    key[25] := 'until     '; key[26] := 'var       ';
    key[27] := 'while     ';
    ksy[ 1] := andsy;        ksy[ 2] := arraysy;
    ksy[ 3] := beginsy;      ksy[ 4] := casesy;
    ksy[ 5] := constsy;      ksy[ 6] := idiv;
    ksy[ 7] := dosy;         ksy[ 8] := downtosy;
    ksy[ 9] := elsesy;       ksy[10] := endsy;
    ksy[11] := forsy;        ksy[12] := funcsy;
    ksy[13] := ifsy;         ksy[14] := imod;
    ksy[15] := notsy;        ksy[16] := ofsy;
    ksy[17] := orsy;         ksy[18] := procsy;
    ksy[19] := programsy;    ksy[20] := recordsy;
    ksy[21] := repeatsy;     ksy[22] := thensy;
    ksy[23] := tosy;         ksy[24] := typesy;
    ksy[25] := untilsy;      ksy[26] := varsy;
    ksy[27] := whilesy;
    sps['+'] := plus;        sps['-'] := minus;
    sps['*'] := times;       sps['/'] := rdiv;
    sps['('] := lparent;     sps[')'] := rparent;
    sps['='] := eql;         sps[','] := comma;
    sps['['] := lbrack;      sps[']'] := rbrack;
    sps[''''] := neq;        sps['!'] := andsy;
    sps[';'] := semicolon;
 end { setup };

 procedure enterids;
```

```
begin
    enter('            ', vvariable, notyp, 0);  { sentinel }
    enter('false       ', konstant, bools, 0);
    enter('true        ', konstant, bools, 1);
    enter('real        ', typel, reals, 1);
    enter('char        ', typel, chars, 1);
    enter('boolean     ', typel, bools, 1);
    enter('integer     ', typel, ints , 1);
    enter('abs         ', funktion, reals,0);
    enter('sqr         ', funktion, reals,2);
    enter('odd         ', funktion, bools,4);
    enter('chr         ', funktion, chars,5);
    enter('ord         ', funktion, ints, 6);
    enter('succ        ', funktion, chars,7);
    enter('pred        ', funktion, chars,8);
    enter('round       ', funktion, ints, 9);
    enter('trunc       ', funktion, ints, 10);
    enter('sin         ', funktion, reals, 11);
    enter('cos         ', funktion, reals, 12);
    enter('exp         ', funktion, reals, 13);
    enter('ln          ', funktion, reals, 14);
    enter('sqrt        ', funktion, reals, 15);
    enter('arctan      ', funktion, reals, 16);
    enter('eof         ', funktion, bools, 17);
    enter('eoln        ', funktion, bools, 18);
    enter('read        ', prozedure, notyp, 1);
    enter('readln      ', prozedure, notyp, 2);
    enter('write       ', prozedure, notyp, 3);
    enter('writeln     ', prozedure, notyp, 4);
    enter('            ', prozedure, notyp, 0);
end;

begin { main }

    setup;

    constbegsys  := [plus,minus,intcon,realcon,charcon,ident];
    typebegsys   := [ident,arraysy,recordsy];
    blockbegsys  := [constsy,typesy,varsy,procsy,funcsy,beginsy];
    facbegsys    := [intcon,realcon,charcon,ident,lparent,notsy];
    statbegsys   := [beginsy,ifsy,whilesy,repeatsy,forsy,casesy];
    stantyps     := [notyp,ints,reals,bools,chars];

        lc := 0;              ll := 0;
        cc := 0;              ch := ' ';
    errpos := 0;            errs := [];

    writeln('NOTE input/output for users program is console: ');
    writeln;

    write('  Source input file ? '); readln(inf);
    reset(psin,inf);

    write('Source listing file ? '); readln(outf);
    rewrite(psout,outf);

    reset(prd,'console:');
    rewrite(prr,'console:');

    insymbol;

        t := -1;              a := 0;
        b := 1;               sx := 0;
        c2 := 0;          display[0] := 1;

        iflag := false;          oflag := false;
     skipflag := false;       prtables:=false;
    stackdump:= false;
```

```
if sy <> programsy
then error(3)
else begin
  insymbol;
  if sy <> ident
  then error(2)
  else begin
    progname := id;
    insymbol;
    if sy <> lparent
    then error(9)
    else repeat
      insymbol;
      if sy <> ident
      then error(2)
      else begin
        if id = 'input
        then iflag := true
        else if id = 'output
              then oflag := true
              else error(0);
        insymbol
      end
    until sy <> comma;

    if sy = rparent then insymbol else error(4);
    if not oflag then error(20)
  end
end ;

enterids;
with btab[1] do
  begin
    last := t; lastpar := l; psize := 0; vsize := 0
  end ;

block(blockbegsys+statbegsys, false, 1);
if sy <> period then error(22);
emit(31);   { halt }

if prtables then printtables;
if errs=[]
then interpret
else begin
  writeln(psout);
  writeln(psout,'compiled with errors');
  writeln(psout);
  errormsg;
end;

writeln(psout);

close(psout,lock);
close(prr  ,lock)

end.
```

10.4 EXAMPLES

The program **MAGIC**, which is used here to illustrate the output of the Pascal S compiler, creates a magic square of order n, that is, an arrangement of the numbers 1 to $n*n$ in a square array, so that the sum of each row and column is the same as the sum of the elements of the two main diagonals. The algorithm given here works for odd values of n only. The number, which appears to the left of each line of the listing, refers to the position in CODE of the first instruction associated with that line. No compiler directives are given by the program.

```
  0     program magic(input,output);
  0
  0     const    maxsize = 11;
  0
  0     type     sqrtype = array [1..maxsize,1..maxsize] of integer;
  0
  0     var      square: sqrtype;
  0              size, row, col  : integer;
  0
  0     procedure makesquare(var sq: sqrtype; limit:integer);
  0
  0     var      num, r, c : integer;
  0
  0     begin
  0        for r:=1 to limit do
  4           for c:=1 to limit do sq[r,c]:=0;
 17
 17        if odd(limit)
 19        then begin  (* start in the middle row of the last column *)
 20           r:=(limit + 1) div 2;
 27           c:=limit;
 30
 30           for num:=1 to sqr(limit) do
 35           begin
 35              if sq[r,c] <> 0
 42              then begin  (* select a different diagonal *)
 44                 r:=r - 1;  if r<1 then r:=r + limit;
 58                 c:=c - 2;  if c<1 then c:=c + limit;
 72              end;
 72              sq[r,c]:=num;  (* number square; move down diagonally to the right *)
 79              r:=r + 1;  if r>limit then r:=r - limit;
 93              c:=c + 1;  if c>limit then c:=c - limit;
107           end; { for }
108
108        end; { if }
108     end; { makesquare }
108
108     begin
109        size:=3;  (* print the 3*3 square anyway *)
112        repeat
112           if (size>2) and (size<12)
118           then begin
120              makesquare(square,size);
124              writeln;
125              for row:=1 to size do
129              begin
129                 for col:=1 to size do write(square[row,col]);
141                 writeln
141              end;
143           end else writeln(' invalid size   - 3..11 only!');;
147
147           read(size)  (* ask for size of next square *)
149        until size=0;
153     end.
```

This program uses the t directive to cause TAB, and other tables, to be printed.

```
 0    program marker(input,output);
 0    {$t+ }
 0
 0    const    classmax = 50;
 0             submax   =  9;
 0
 0    type     profile = record
 0                         reference : integer;
 0                         checked   : boolean;
 0                         marks     : array [1..submax] of integer;
 0                         grade     : integer;
 0                       end;
 0             formtyp = array [1..classmax] of profile;
 0
 0    var     klass: formtyp;
 0
 0    procedure grader(var class: formtyp);
 0
 0    var      pupil, subject, marks, exams: integer;
 0
 0    begin
 0      for pupil:=1 to classmax do
 4      begin
 4        if class[pupil].checked
 8        then begin
10          marks:=0;        exams:=0;
16          for subject:=1 to submax do
20            if class[pupil].marks[subject] >= 0
28            then begin  (*compute total marks and number of exams*)
30              marks:=marks + class[pupil].marks[subject];
41              exams:=exams + 1
44            end;
47          class[pupil].grade:=(marks div exams) div 10
55        end
57      end { for pupil }
57    end; { grader    }
58
58    begin
59         { no body }
59    end.
```

Ø TAB

identifiers	link	obj	typ	ref	nrm	lev	adr
28	27	3	0	2	1	0	59
29 classmax	0	0	1	0	0	1	50
30 submax	29	0	1	0	0	1	9
31 profile	30	2	6	3	0	1	12
32 reference	0	1	1	0	1	2	0
33 checked	32	1	3	0	1	2	1
34 marks	33	1	5	1	1	2	2
35 grade	34	1	1	0	1	2	11
36 formtyp	31	2	5	2	0	1	600
37 klass	36	1	5	2	1	1	5
38 grader	37	3	0	4	1	1	0
39 class	0	1	5	2	0	2	5
40 pupil	39	1	1	0	1	2	6
41 subject	40	1	1	0	1	2	7
42 marks	41	1	1	0	1	2	8
43 exams	42	1	1	0	1	2	9

blocks	last	lpar	psze	vsze
1	28	1	0	0
2	38	28	5	605
3	35	0	0	12
4	43	39	6	10

arrays	xtyp	etyp	eref	low	high	elsz	size
1	1	1	0	1	9	1	9
2	1	6	3	1	50	12	600

The compile time error messages produced by Pascal S are brief but pertinent. They could usefully and easily be made longer. This has not been done in the version of the system given here because increasing the length of the error message strings means increasing the storage requirements of the compiler. Since the system listed here is usually used in an environment where memory is limited, the message strings have been kept brief. Where memory is plentiful, the messages could and should be extended.

```
    0    program magicerrs(input,output);
    0
    0    const    maxsize = 11;
    0
    0    type     sqrtype = array [maxsize,maxsize] of integer;
****                                  ↑13        ↑13
    0
    0    var      square: sqrtype;
    0             size, row, col   : integer;
    0
    0    procedure makesquare(var sq: sqrtype; limit:integer);
    0
    0    var    r, c : integer;
    0
    0    begin
    0      for i:=1 to limit do
****           ↑ 0
    3        for c:=1 to limit do sq[r,c]:=0;
   16
   16      r:=(limit + 1) div 2;
   23      c:=n;
****         ↑ 0
   25
   25      for num:=1 to sqr(limit) do
****             ↑ 0
   29      begin
   29        if sq[i,j] <> 0
****                 ^ 0
   34        then begin
   36          r:=r - 1;       c:=c - 2;
   46          if r<1 then r:=r + limit;
   55          if c<1 then c:=c + limit;
   64        end;
   64        sq[r,c]:=num;
****                   ^ 0
   70        r:=r + 1;      if r>limit then r:=r - limit;
   84        c:=c + 1;      if c>limit then c:=c - limit;
   98      end; { for }
   99    end; { makesquare }
   99
   99    begin
```

```
100      size:=3;
103      repeat
103        if size>2 and size<12
****                       ↑ 6
107        then begin
****            ↑32
109        writeln;
110        for row:=1 to limit do
****                        ↑ 0
114        begin
114          for col:=1 to limit do write(square[row,col])
****                          ↑ 0
125        writeln
****             ↑14
125        end;
127      end else writeln(' invalid size  - 3..11 only!');;
131
131      read(size)
133      until size=0;
137   end.
```

compiled with errors

  key words

0   undef id

6   syntax

13 ..

14 ;

32 boole type

10.5 Pascal S .. ERROR SUMMARY

0 undefined identifier

1 attempt at multiple definition

2 identifier expected (but not found)

3 'program' expected but not found

4 ')' expected but not found

5 ':' expected but not found

6 illegal symbol

7 error in formal parameter list

8 'of' expected

9 '(' expected

10 type error

11 '[' expected

12 ']' expected

13 '..' expected

14 ';' expected

15 error in function result type

16 '=' expected

17 expression must have boolean result

18 control variable must be of type variable

19 type conflict between control variable and expression

20 error in program parameter list

21   number too large
22   '.' expected
23   invalid expression type following case
24   illegal character
25   identifier of type constant expected
26   array index type conflict
27   type conflict in declaration of array index bounds
28   no such array
29   error in type of identifier
30   undefined type
31   no such record
32   boolean type expected
33   arithmetic type expected
34   integer type expected
35   invalid operator
36   actual/formal parameter type conflict
37   item must be of type variable
38   string expected
39   not enough actual parameters
40   no digits after decimal point
41   incorrect type
42   type real expected
43   integer expected
44   variable of constant expected
45   variable of procedure identifier expected
46   type conflict in operands
47   label type incompatible with selecting expression
48   incorrect type of expression for standard function
49   store overflow
50   constant expected-
51   ':=' expected
52   'then' expected
53   'until' expected
54   'do' expected
55   'to' or 'downto' expected
56   'begin' expected -
57   'end' expected
58   factor expected

Chapter 11

Pascal S Interpreter

It is only in the procedure INTERPRET that the run time stack is defined. The size of the stack will of course determine the amount of storage space, and work space, available to a program processed by Pascal S. The Pascal S program itself, together with the work space it requires, makes considerable demands on machines with memories of 32k words. The table sizes, given in the listing of Pascal S, have been chosen to enable the program to be used on such machines as Data General Nova (using the Lancaster P4 Pascal), the Apple II, and Western Digital Microengine (using UCSD Pascal). If lack of memory is a problem, then it is straightforward to separate the interpreter from the compiler and run each independently. If this is done, then the information generated by the compiler can be written to filestore and subsequently read by the interpreter program. The data which needs to be transferred is

CODE   the code to be interpreted,
BTAB   the block table,
TAB   the symbol table,
ATAB   the array table,
RCONST   the table of real constants,
STAB   the table of strings.

In addition the size of each table must be given. More economical use of memory can also be achieved by using the procedure INTERPRET as an overlay, or a segment procedure, which is only resident in memory when it is being used.

INTERPRET is a large procedure but its action is easy to understand. The body of the procedure is dominated by the <u>case</u> statement which uses the operation code of each instruction as the case statement selector. This means that the instructions necessary to implement each of the Pascal S operation codes are easy to follow. An understanding of the run time stack organisation is essential to an understanding of INTERPRET.

11.1 THE RUN TIME STACK

We shall say that there will be one stack frame associated with each block of the source program. Its structure is given diagrammatically in Figure 11.1.

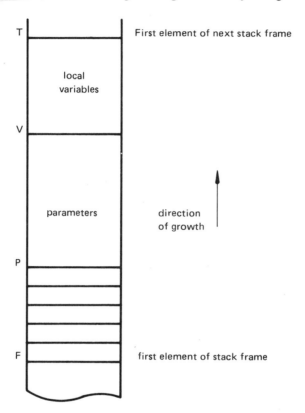

for a typical stack frame

V−F = PSZE
T−F = VSZE
P−F =   5   ~   the number of storage units required for housekeeping
V−P =   ~   the number of storage units required for parameters
T−V =   ~   the number of storage units required for variables local to this procedure function.

Fig. 11.1 − A typical stack frame.

Every procedure call in the source program causes the construction and use of a new stack frame. In order that the transition from one stack frame to another be done in an orderly fashion, two low level instructions are used: MARK and CALL. As soon as a procedure call is recognised a MARK instruction is generated. The effect of this instruction at run time is illustrated in Figure 11.2.

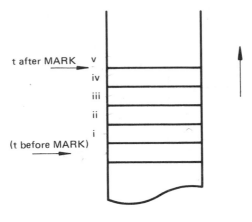

t is the top of stack pointer

Fig. 11.2 — Effect of the MARK instruction.

Space for five housekeeping cells is created on the stack by moving the stack pointer 't'. The five cells numbered will ultimately have contents as follows:

    i) function result
    ii) code position of call, 'pc'
    iii) static link
    iv) dynamic link
    v) position in TAB of procedure identifier

Only two locations are used by MARK, those numbered iv, and v. Of these iv is used as a temporary and only v is given the value as indicated above.

Between the generation of MARK, and its matching CALL, the parameter list is processed by the compiler. This means that instructions will be generated to evaluate all the parameters of the procedure. The result of this is to leave either the values or the addresses of the parameters required on the stack. Only after all parameters have been dealt with is the CALL instruction for the procedure generated.

In this way all values local to one procedure call are available in the relevant stack frame. The top of the stack can be used for the manipulation of data as prescribed by the procedure.

On exit from the procedure the stack pointer resumes the value it had immediately before the MARK instruction, except in the case of a function. A function will leave its result on the stack. On exit from a function the stack pointer 't' will have a value one greater than it had immediately before MARK.

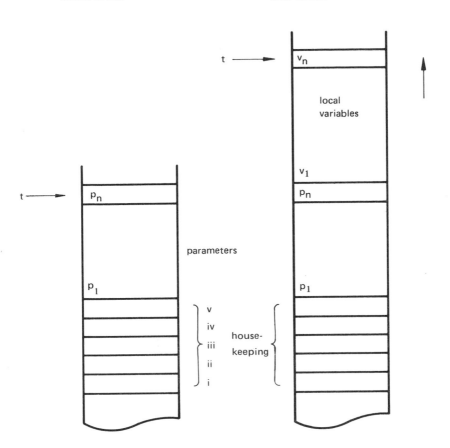

Fig. 11.3 — After the CALL instruction the static storage allocation is complete.

The stack 'snapshots', given with several programs, are obtained by using the s directive to print the stack contents on procedure entry. Note that only the integer variant of the record which is each stack element is printed.

The example below uses a recursive procedure 'octalout' to illustrate the behaviour of the run time stack. The stack snapshots are obtained as part of the processing associated with the call of the procedure.

```
* 0    program octalprint(input, output);
  0    {$s+ }
  0
  0    var    decimal: integer;
  0
  0    procedure octalout(number: integer);
  0
  0    begin
  0      if number<8
  2      then write(number:1)
  7      else begin
  8        octalout(number div 8);
 14        write(number mod 8:1)
 19      end
 19    end; { octalout }
 19
 19    begin
 20      write('? '); read(decimal);
 24
 24      while decimal>0 do
 28      begin
 28        write(decimal:6,' ':6);
 34        octalout(decimal);
 37        writeln;
 38        write('? '); read(decimal)
 42      end
 42    end.
```

              calling octalout
                   level   1
          start of code   0

contents of display

      1   0
      0   0

top of stack   11   frame base   6

                   stack contents

                   11   120   parameter value
                   10   30
                    9   0
                    8   0
                    7   37
                    6   32   ⟨———— start of frame .. first call
                    5   120
                    4   28
                    3   −1
                    2   0
                    1   0
                   ⟨ =   =   = ⟩

              calling octalout
                   level   1
          start of code   0

contents of display

1	0
0	0

top of stack   17   frame base   12

stack contents

17	15	parameter value
16	30	
15	6	
14	0	
13	13	
12	−2	⟨−−−− start of frame .. second call
11	120	
10	30	
9	0	
8	0	
7	37	
6	32	⟨−−−− start of frame .. first call
5	120	
4	28	
3	−1	
2	0	
1	0	
⟨ =	= = ⟩	

calling octalout
level   1
start of code   0

contents of display

1	0
0	0

top of stack   23   frame base   18

stack contents

23	1	parameter value
22	30	
21	12	
20	0	
19	13	
18	−2	⟨−−−− frame base .. third call
17	15	
16	30	

15	6
14	0
13	13
12	−2 ⟨−−−− frame base .. second call
11	120
10	30
9	0
8	0
7	37
6	32 ⟨−−−− frame base .. first call
5	120
4	28
3	−1
2	0
1	0
⟨ = = = ⟩	

11.2 The role of DISPLAY at run time

The value associated with an identifier of, say, type integer is accessed at run time using a level number and an offset. Assuming that the program is at level zero, the level number, or static level, is obtained by incrementing the level number at the start of each block, and decrementing it at the end of each block in a lexicographic scan of the program. The level number identifies the stack frame associated with the block in which the identifier was defined. The offset gives the displacement from the base of the stack frame. The array DISPLAY holds the stack frame base for each of the static levels below the current level. The level number is used as an index into DISPLAY.

When a procedure (or function) is called, the frame base is inserted into DISPLAY after retrieving the level number of the procedure from TAB. Leaving a procedure may involve a rather bigger overhead. In leaving a procedure declared at level one, we may be returning to a procedure declared at a higher level. If this happens, then part of the work undertaken in leaving the procedure must be the recreation of the contents of DISPLAY. This work is carried out by the 'update display' instruction of the interpreter. That this updating is necessary can be established by considering the rather contrived program which follows. For brevity the contents of the stack have been suppressed.

N level

```
 0    program leveller(output);
 0    {$s+ }
 0
 0    procedure level1a;
 0      procedure level2a;
 0        procedure level3a;
 0        begin
 0          writeln('level 3a')
 2        end; { level3a }
 3      begin
 4        level3a
 4      end; { level2a }
 6    begin
 7      level2a
 7    end; { level1a }
 9
 9    procedure level1b;
10      procedure level2b;
10        procedure level3b;
10          procedure level4b;
10          begin
10            writeln(' level 4b')
12          end; { level4b }
13        begin
14          level1a;
17          level4b
17        end; { level3b }
19      begin
20        level3b
20      end; { level2b }
22    begin
23      level2b
23    end; { level1b }
25
25    begin
26      level1b
26    end.
```

loop1
loop2
loop3
loop4

            calling level1b
                level   1
        start of code   23

contents of display

    1   0
    0   0

top of stack   9   frame base   5

        ****

            calling level2b
                level   2
        start of code   20

contents of display

    2   5
    1   0
    0   0

top of stack   14   frame base   10

        ****

                    calling level3b
                        level   3
            start of code   14

contents of display

  3   10
  2.   5
  1   0
  0   0

top of stack   19   frame base   15

            ****

                    calling level1a
                        level   1
            start of code   7

contents of display

  1   0
  0   0

top of stack   24   frame base   20

            ****

                    calling level2a
                        level   2
            start of code   4

contents of display

  2   20
  1   0
  0   0

top of stack   29   frame base   25

            ****

                    calling level3a
                        level   3
            start of cod   0

contents of display

  3   25
  2   20
  1   0
  0   0

top of stack   34   frame base   30

            ****

                    calling level4b
                          level   4
               start of code   10

contents of display
          4   15
          3   10
          2   5
          1   0
          0   0

top of stack   24   frame base   20

In the program PMDUMP an error has been introduced to cause a run time failure. As a result the output from the post mortem dump can be shown.


```
 0   program pmdump(output);
 0   {$s- }
 0
 0   procedure level1a;
 0     procedure level2a;
 0       procedure level3a;
 0       begin
 0         writeln('level 3a');
 3         writeln('force an error', 3 div 0:4)
10       end; { level3a }
11     begin
12       level3a
12     end; { level2a }
14   begin
15     level2a
15   end; { level1a }
17
17   procedure level1b;
18     procedure level2b;
18       procedure level3b;
18         procedure level4b;
18         begin
18           writeln(' level 4b')
20         end; { level4b }
21       begin
22         level1a; { snap 2 }
25         level4b   { snap 3 }
25       end; { level3b }
27     begin
28       level3b     { snap 1 }
28     end; { level2b }
30   begin
31     level2b
31   end; { level1b }
33
33   begin
34     level1b
34   end.
```

level 3a
force an error
      halt at   8 because of division by 0
      level3a   called at 14
      level2a   called at 17
      level1a   called at 24
      level3b   called at 30
      level2b   called at 33
      level1b   called at 36

Zellers congruence allows the day associated with a given date to be computed. Given a date in the form day, month, year, the program Zeller uses a slightly modified form of the congruence to compute the day on which this date falls. The day is represented by an integer in the range 0..6 where 0 represents Sunday. This program illustrates code produced by Pascal S.

```
 0    program zeller(input,output);
 0    {$t+ }
 0    var        day, month, year,
 0               zday, m, y1, y2 : integer;
 0
 0    begin
 0       read(day,month,year);
 6       if month < 3
 8       then begin
10          m:=month + 10;
15          year:=year-1
18       end else
20          m:=month - 2;
26
26       y1:=year div 100;
31       y2:=year mod 100;
36
36       zday:=(day + trunc(2.6*m - 0.1)
45                   + y2 + y2 div 4
50                   + y1 div 4 - 2*y1 +49) mod 7;
65
65       write(zday)
67    end.
```

identifiers	link	obj	typ	ref	nrm	lev	adr
28	27	3	0	2	1	0	0
29 day	0	1	1	0	1	1	5
30 month	29	1	1	0	1	1	6
31 year	30	1	1	0	1	1	7
32 zday	31	1	1	0	1	1	8
33 m	32	1	1	0	1	1	9
34 y1	33	1	1	0	1	1	10
35 y2	34	1	1	0	1	1	11

blocks	last	1par	psze	vsze
1	28	1	0	0
2	35	28	5	12

code:

code	f	x	y	code	f	x	y
0	0	1	5,	35	38		,
1	27		1,	36	0	1	8,
2	0	1	6,	37	1	1	5,
3	27		1,	38	25		1,
4	0	1	7,	39	1	1	9,
5	27		1,	40	26		0,
6	1	1	6,	41	60		,
7	24		3, 1	42	25		2,
8	47		,	43	55		,
9	11		21, 25	44	8		10,
10	0	1	9,	45	52		,
11	1	1	6,	46	1	1	11,
12	24		10,	47	52		,
13	52		,	48	1	1	11,
14	38		,	49	24		4,
15	0	1	7,	50	58		,
16	1	1	7,	51	52		,
17	24		1,	52	1	1	10,
18	53		,	53	24		4,
19	38		,	54	58		,
20	10		26, 7	55	52		,
21	0	1	9,	56	24		2,
22	1	1	6,	57	1	1	10,
23	24		2,	58	57		,
24	53		,	59	53		,
25	38		,	60	24		49,
26	0	1	10,	61	52		,
27	1	1	7,	62	24		7,
28	24		100,	63	59		,
29	58		,	64	38		,
30	38		,	65	1	1	8,
31	0	1	11,	66	29		1,
32	1	1	7,	67	31		,
33	24		100,				
34	59		,				

Starting address is 0

11.3 PASCAL S OPERATION CODES

Code	x	y	Action
0	x	y	Load address
1	x	y	Load value
2	x	y	Load indirect

3	x	y	Update DISPLAY
4			not used ·
5			not used
6			not used
7			not used
8		y	Standard functions (selected by y 0 .. 18)
9		y	Add y to the element on top of the stack
10		y	Jump to y (unconditional)
11		y	Jump to y if stack top false
12		y	Jump to y (case table) and select entry
13		y	Entry in case table ... NOT EXECUTABLE
14		y	For loop entry test – UP
15		y	For loop retry test – UP
16		y	For loop entry test – DOWN
17		y	For loop retry test – DOWN
18		y	Mark stack
19		y	Call user procedure
20		y	Indexed fetch (element size 〈〉 1)
21		y	Indexed fetch
22		y	Load block
23		y	Copy block
24		y	Load literal
25		y	Load real
26		y	Float
27		y	Read (y denotes type .. 1 integer, 2 real, 3 boolean)
28		y	Write string
29		y	Write .. default field widths
30		y	Write .. given field widths
31			HALT
32			Exit procedure
33			Exit function
34			Fetch
35			Not
36			Negate
37			Write real .. given field widths
38			Store
39			Real =
40			Real 〈〉
41			Real 〈
42			Real 〈=
43			Real 〉
44			Real 〉=
45			Integer =

46	Integer ⟨⟩
47	Integer ⟨
48	Integer ⟨=
49	Integer ⟩
50	Integer ⟩=
51	Or
52	+ integer
53	− integer
54	+ real
55	− real
56	And
57	* integer
58	Div
59	Mod
60	* real
61	/
62	Read1n
63	Write1n

Index